Let the little children come to me,
and do not hinder them,
for the kingdom of God
belongs to such as these.

THE GOSPELS & ACTS

JOEL B. GREEN

INTERVARSITY PRESS
DOWNERS GROVE, ILLINOIS 60515

©1987 by InterVarsity Christian Fellowship of the United States of America.

InterVarsity Press is the book-publishing division of InterVarsity Christian Fellowship, a student movement active on campus at hundreds of universities, colleges and schools of nursing. For information about local and regional activities, write Public Relations Dept., InterVarsity Christian Fellowship, 6400 Schroeder Rd., P.O. Box 7895, Madison, WI 53707-7895.

Distributed in Canada through InterVarsity Press, 860 Denison St., Unit 3, Markham, Ontario L3R 4H1, Canada.

Cover illustration: Roberta Polfus

ISBN 0-87784-940-4

Printed in the United States of America

British Library Cataloguing in Publication Data

Green, Joel B.
  How to read the Gospels and Acts.
  [How to read series]
  1. Bible. N.T. Gospels-Commentaries
  2. Bible. N.T. Acts-Commentaries
  I. Title
  226'.06   BS2555.3

ISBN 0-85110-776-1

Library of Congress Cataloging in Publication Data

Green, Joel B., 1956-
  How to read the Gospels & Acts.

  (How to read series)
  Bibliography: p.
  Includes index.
  1. Bible. N.T. Gospels—Study. 2. Bible. N.T.
Acts—Study. I. Title. II. Series.
BS2556.G74   226'.061   87-5572
ISBN 0-87784-940-4

17	16	15	14	13	12	11	10	9	8	7	6	5	4	3	2	1
99	98	97	96	95	94	93	92	91	90	89	88	87				

THE HOW TO READ SERIES

The Bible is one book, yet it consists of many—history and wisdom,
prophecy and apocalyptic, poetry and letters, law and narrative.
This variety, while it enriches us, also challenges us. How
are we to comprehend the unique contribution each type of literature makes
to our understanding of God and our world?

The How to Read series is designed for nonprofessionals who want
a professional understanding of Scripture. Each volume is
written by an expert and focuses on one type of biblical literature,
explaining its unique features and how these features should shape the way
we approach it. The goal throughout is to help us all better
understand the Bible and apply it to our lives.

Available now:

How to Read the Bible by A. J. Conyers
How to Read Prophecy by Joel Green
How to Read the Gospels & Acts by Joel Green

Forthcoming:

How to Read the Psalms

To Aaron and Allison

Preface

I have always thought of myself as an ordinary Christian. What appeals to me doubtless appeals to others. Imagine my shock, then, when a close friend confided, "Actually, Joel, I never read the Gospels." To me the Gospels are the wellsprings of the good news. To her the parables are riddles, the meaning of the Gospels obscured in the mists of time. "Give me the letters of Paul," she said. "Those I can understand."

This book is an invitation. An invitation to my friend and others like her. An invitation to look again at the Gospels and Acts.

Like the others in the How to Read series this book is not a commentary. Nor is it a full-blown introduction to the message of these important books of the Bible. Rather, I have tried to chart the lay of the land for studying the Gospels and Acts—the nature of these writings, the background they presuppose, and the way they embody the good news. For those who desire to delve further into the issues presented here, I have included a suggested reading list at the close of the book. In the majority of instances, biblical quotations follow the New International Version, though on occasion I have provided my own translation.

It is both a necessity and privilege to record my gratitude to the many friends who have interacted with me on much of the substance of this book. My greatest appreciation must be addressed to my family—Pam, Aaron and Allison—for their partnership in the rather topsy-turvy transition period during which this book was written. I should also mention Bill Dyrness and Peggy Parker, who read all or part of this material in an earlier form; to Paul Ellingworth, for his encouragement at the seminal stages of this book; and to Howard Marshall and David Millikan, whose diverse influences continually push me to a truly Christian reading of the Gospels and Acts.

PART I
Approaching
the
Gospels

1
An Introduction to Reading the Gospels

"Jesus is Lord." These three words form the earliest confession uniting Jesus' disciples from the beginning of Christianity.[1] With these words, Christians assert that the same person that was born in Bethlehem, ministered in ancient Palestine and was crucified under Pontius Pilate, rules eternally. It is only natural, then, that followers of the Risen Lord, ancient and modern, are drawn repeatedly to the Gospels which tell us of Jesus' earthly ministry.

In them we read of the most exciting and mysterious happening—God himself openly declares his solidarity with men and women, indeed, with all creation in an unprecedented way. He is Immanuel, God with us. He becomes as we are, lives among us, rejoices and suffers with us. All of this he does with us and for us, for our salvation. In the Gospels the message of redemption appears as no ivory-tower philosophy. Good news is presented as no mere set of ideas, no list of propositions. It breathes; it walks and talks; it is a man, Jesus of Nazareth. Here God intervenes in real, this-worldly history. Here is a marvelous story, full of life and vitality, to which men and women across the centuries have been drawn again and again.

Yet, by the second century, doubt was cast on the value of the Gospels for Christian faith. At that early juncture in the church's history, Marcion discerned the "pure gospel" in the letters of Paul. Because of Luke's traditional association with Paul, only his Gospel (and an edited version at that!) survived in Marcion's list of authoritative Christian writings. The other three Gospels were rejected. Of course, we know that Marcion's attempt to define the Christian message solely in Pauline terms was not successful, but the spirit of Marcion lives on in some quarters. Indeed, in some Protestant circles today, Paul's epistles continue to be regarded as the most sure deposit of Christian truth. In part, this results from the temptation to read the Bible through the lens provided by the Reformation emphasis on justification by faith, and Paul stresses this idea more than any other writer. A more practical reason probably lies behind the modern reincarnation of Marcion's proposal, however.

Simply put, many feel uneasy in trying to understand the message of the Gospels. Contemporary Christians often find the letters of the New Testament easier to read. The epistles, it is presumed, yield their truth more easily, more directly than the sometimes enigmatic sayings and stories of the Gospels. Our textbook-and-lecture-oriented educational system places a high value on factual data, logic, objective thought and rationalistic prose. It is no wonder that the Gospels often seem like books from an alien world, shrouded in mystery. Indeed, at times they appear to raise more questions than answers.

Why include those boring genealogies? How can the dead bury the dead? Why don't the Gospel accounts agree with one another? What is this talk about pearls and mustard seeds? Must I really hate my mother and father? What could Jesus possibly have been thinking?

There can be no denying that the Gospels present us with a few problems. This is true for a variety of reasons—not the least of which centers on the fact that the Gospels constitute a form of literature for which there are very few parallels. What is the nature of the Gospels? How should they be read as pieces of literature and as Scripture? These are fundamental questions confronting modern Christians. Closely related issues include: Why *four* Gospels rather than a single, authoritative account? What are we to make of the differences, minor and major, between Gospel stories? Do the Gospels tell us "what really happened"?

A closer examination of the Gospels suggests other significant questions of interpretation. A variety of linguistic and narrative tools are employed by the Gospel writers. Many of these devices stretch the categories we are accustomed to in our reading. Parables, for example, rarely appear in our newspapers or sports magazines. College essays and business reports are unlikely to take on the look of a collage of Old Testament texts, but this is precisely what we find in the birth and passion narratives of the four Gospels. Jesus' sayings appear in the Gospels in garb that may not be readily recognizable to us—and an attempt to take all of them at face value might be misdirected.

Finally, there is the keynote of Jesus' message, an understanding of which is vital to any reading of the Gospels. No framework can be imported from outside the Gospels for coming to terms with their central concerns. Only the message of Jesus can serve this function. What is this keynote? The kingdom of God is the hub of Jesus' message, and no serious reader of the Gospels can get far without understanding this concept.

Students of the Gospels can benefit from discussions of all these major concerns. In fact, these are the very issues we will look at together in the following chapters. At this point, however, we would do well to ask an even more fundamental question. What can we hope to gain from our reading of the Gospels? What do the Gospels "do" for us? Of the many possible responses to this question I will mention four of the most important.

A Historical Faith
In the first place we must note that the Gospels, more than any of the other New Testament writings, ground our faith in real history. The Gospel writers, though, were not always interested in the details of history, nor were they interested in history

simply for the sake of history. Rather, they were convinced that something extraordinary had taken place *at a certain time* and *at a certain place*. And this "extraordinary something" could not be captured in mere creedal statements or slogans.

This man Jesus, in whom God had acted once for all, could not be reduced to a certain Christological title or dogmatic assertion. Indeed, if this "event" had simply become the content of a confession, God would be known only as some sort of ghost, an abstract being somewhere "out there." But this is not the God whom those early Christians experienced in Jesus. Here was a human life which seemed more than human. For this reason those early evangelists told a story, *his* story, the story of the coming of the Messiah of God. Only in story could the significance of this man and his mission be related. This life could never be condensed into a formula.

So, for example, instead of writing a theological treatise or confessional tract, Luke wrote a Gospel. Instead of creating a new formula by which to assert the kernel of Jesus' mission, Luke told a certain story. This was the story of Jesus' encounter with Zacchaeus the tax collector: How Zacchaeus, having heard of Jesus' coming, climbed a sycamore-fig tree that he might see Jesus walking by. . . . How Jesus saw Zacchaeus and invited himself to dinner. . . . How Zacchaeus was subsequently moved to give half of his possessions to the poor and to repay at a highly inflated interest rate anything he had taken dishonestly. . . . How Jesus pronounced salvation on the house of Zacchaeus, "because this man, too, is a son of Abraham." Through this story we come to understand Jesus' words "for the Son of Man came to seek and to save the lost" (Lk 19:10 RSV). This is no abstract truth but a living reality set in the context of Jesus' daily ministry. In this way the day-to-day life of Jesus, culminating in his death and resurrection, provides the context in which we understand his significance.[2]

In so closely tying the *meaning* of Jesus together to his *story*, those early Christians were only following in the well-worn path of their Jewish ancestors in the faith. The earliest Christians would have been Jews and Gentile proselytes. As such they would have had history in their blood, for in history Israel had come to experience God and understood his character. And in *this* history—the story of Jesus' ministry, death and resurrection—those early Christians saw God moving in an extraordinary way. Their faith could never be separated from that story. Neither can ours.

Knowing Jesus

As Christians, then, our faith is inseparably wrapped up in Jesus of Nazareth. If, as some have tried to argue, Jesus never really existed, this would create far-reaching problems for the Christian movement. Similarly, if we could know nothing of Jesus beyond the fact of his existence, then we would know very little about what it might mean to follow him as disciples.

Of course, we have no record of Jesus' ever having written a book or published a sermon. History has left us no directly autobiographical material from Jesus. Living as we do some two thousand years after the birth of Jesus, we must face the impossibility of our knowing anything of this man from Nazareth by direct observation. For such information we are totally dependent on the reports of others. In this respect we are no different than many first-century believers—those who came to faith without having known the man Jesus. Their faith, however, was in no way inferior to the faith of those who had first walked and talked with Jesus. In fact, it was just such later-generation Christians that John had in mind when he included in his Gospel the words of Jesus to Thomas: "Because you have seen me, you have believed; blessed are those who have not seen and yet have believed" (Jn 20:29 NIV).

Because we are later-generation Christians we may be all the more grateful for the Gospels, for in them we have our most direct witness to Jesus of Nazareth. Outside of these first four books of our New Testament there is a remarkable paucity of information about the man Jesus. To be sure, Paul knows the tradition of the Last Supper (1 Cor 11:23-25) and even quotes a saying of Jesus (1 Cor 7:10), Hebrews seems to record something of the prayer-struggle of Jesus on the night of his betrayal

(Heb 5:7), and 1 Timothy 6:13 appeals to the example of Jesus before Pilate. On the whole, however, apart from the evangelists, the New Testament writers seem to assume for their readers a basic familiarity with the story of Jesus.

The Gospels, then, in a unique and vastly important way, bring us in touch with Jesus of Nazareth, even as they interpret the significance of his work and words for first-century Christians.

The Lasting Significance of Jesus

In the ancient world, stories of extraordinary men and women were often told. In this way great heroes and heroines of the past were paraded before successive generations as examples and models. We must be clear about this, however. Telling the story of Jesus was for those early Christians *not* a form of hero worship. My previous comments have focused on the importance of the past—the necessity of a particular history, Jesus' story, for Christian faith. My third comment moves us forward from this orientation, for we find in the Gospels a message and challenge of enduring relevance. We find here the story of a man in whom ultimate significance is embodied.

The very fact that the Gospels came to be written supports this idea. In writing the First Gospel, Matthew was saying, in effect: This story about Jesus is more than a story about a few selected years in world history; this story has relevance for me and for my Christian community. This story encounters us where we live. This story has something to say about how we live before God. We need to keep hearing and learning from this story.

In the same way this story exercises a mysterious power over Christians in this and every century. Even though it appears in four different versions; even though it bespeaks a world far removed chronologically, culturally and geographically from our own; even though it uses literary forms with which we must struggle; we, like Matthew and his fellow Christians, find in this story something of ultimate significance.

The Jesus of the Gospels continues to speak through that

story. Through them he addresses us. Through them he lays his claim on our lives. Through them he reaches out to us with divine love.

Setting the Contours

Finally, and closely related to my third comment, the Gospels provide the historical arena in which the Christian life is lived. That is, being Christian is being related to Christ. And how we are to be related to Christ is expounded to an important degree in the Gospels. We can illustrate this idea with a couple of examples from the Gospel of Mark.

First, in Mark 10:1-12 we learn an important lesson about what we might call "life in the middle." In this passage we see a distinction made between three "times." There is, we are told, a time "at the beginning of creation," when the marriage bond was inseparable. There is, further, a time of "hardness of heart," during which "Moses permitted a man to write a certificate of divorce and send [his wife] away." There is, finally, a new time, a time when hardness of heart is overcome and the original ideal of marriage is again upheld.

We must ask, What has made the difference? How can a "new time" be introduced? How can Jesus overstep the Mosaic regulation? What new factor has entered into the formula? The answer seems clear: Jesus has come—and with him the long-expected time (Mk 1:14-15). With this new possibilities are made available.

On the other hand, inasmuch as in Mark 10:10-11 Jesus goes on to talk about subsequent divorces, he admits that in spite of his coming, "hardness of heart" will continue. Divorce, as illogical as it might seem, will still take place. Divorce (and with it, we might add, other acts which work against God's order), in light of Jesus' coming, is now "out of date." Nevertheless, the end has not yet come, we are not living in the eschaton, and hardness of heart still persists. We are living, then, "in the middle," in tension, during the period of overlap between hardness of heart and new creation.

During this life "in the middle" we are *called* to live according to the ideals of the inbreaking kingdom of God in the presence of the human predicament, in spite of the persistence of sin. And we are *enabled* to do so precisely because of the inbreaking kingdom of God, because Jesus has come and opened up this new possibility.

Without delving in any deep way in Mark 2:23-28, we want to look briefly at these verses in order to further illustrate how the Gospels set the contours for Christian life. We see in this story how Jesus pointed his finger at the prevailing religious attitudes of his contemporaries—and how he continues to do the same. It will be helpful to have this whole passage in view:

One Sabbath Jesus was going through the grainfields, and as his disciples walked along, they began to pick some heads of grain. The Pharisees said to him, "Look, why are they doing what is unlawful on the Sabbath?"

He answered, "Have you never read what David did when he and his companions were hungry and in need? In the days of Abiathar the high priest, he entered the house of God and ate the consecrated bread, which is lawful only for the priests to eat. And he also gave some to his companions."

Then he said to them, "The Sabbath was made for man, not man for the Sabbath. So the Son of Man is Lord even of the Sabbath." (NIV)

Our understanding of this text will be enhanced if we fill in a little background to this narrated event:

1. During the time of Jesus strict observance of the Sabbath was a sign of taking holiness seriously. It was a kind of litmus test for faithfulness to God.

2. Since Jesus and his disciples apparently had no way to prepare their Sabbath meal in advance nor the wherewithal to preserve food from one day to the next even if they had it to preserve, and since they were plucking heads of grain from someone else's field, we can justifiably conclude from this text that they were experiencing no little poverty. In eating from the leftovers, Jesus and his disciples were taking advantage of Old Testament legislation like Deuteronomy 24:19-22 or Leviticus 19:9-10, which gave the poor the right to share in the harvest.

3. In the eyes of the professors and preachers of their day, then, Jesus and his disciples were both poor and unfaithful to God.

4. Nevertheless, Jesus takes it upon himself to place *his* interpretation of the Old Testament over against those whose learning and holiness were above question! His reading of the Scriptures began from the standpoint that the law of God was an expression of the character of God—the character of the one who had heard Israel crying out under Egyptian oppression and had responded (see, for example, Ex 20:1). According to this interpretation, above all else stood basic human need.

For some this story may not seem to speak very directly to our day. However, if we allow it to do so, this story may very well explode many of our preconceptions about Jesus and holiness.

For example, I remember well my initial shock when our son went up to a department-store Santa Claus in Oakland, California. Protruding from those red-Santa sleeves were black hands. Santa's face was black, too. Santa was a black man! How could this be? Naturally, or so I had thought, Santa Claus would be a *white* man with a *white* beard who spoke with my kind of accent. In the same way, we often remake Jesus in our own image—and this Gospel portrait of Jesus as a wholly unacceptable man religiously, socially and economically may well shock us. He was not the sort of fellow, the all-American male, for whom we might want to write a letter of reference. He was definitely not youth pastor material. In this story he appears as a religious reject, a person on the fringes of acceptable behavior.

Similarly, we, like the Pharisees of our story, have our own ideas about what it means to be holy. Many Christians today associate faithfulness to God with church attendance, serving on evangelism or worship committees, and having a quiet time. Like keeping the Sabbath in Jesus' day, these are not in themselves bad things. But they are not *the* thing! To rephrase Jesus' words, "Quiet time was made for men and women, not men and women for quiet time."

Conclusion

The message of the Gospels, then, is not always a reassuring message. Sometimes their stories challenge us. Always, however, in them lies the potential for us to hear a message, a message from God. In this chapter we have both seen the import of reading the Gospels and come face to face with some of the issues behind a serious reading of these four books. From here we embark on a path through these concerns as we attempt to grapple with the nature and interpretation of the Gospels and Acts.

2
One Gospel— Four Gospels

An evangelist-friend of mine devoted many months to building a genuine friendship with a Japanese couple in his community. In the course of their conversation one day he encouraged them to look more fully into the historical roots of the Christian faith by reading the New Testament. After a few days of reading the four Gospels, the wife surprised my friend with her pressing question, "But why did Jesus have to die four times?"

To persons raised in the church or otherwise acquainted with the Bible, this must seem a silly question. Yet it raises abruptly a forceful issue for readers of the·Gospels. Why four accounts? Why four different versions? Why four distinct perspectives? Why not only one, authoritative account? Here is certainly one of the most significant issues confronting readers of the first four books of our New Testament: There are four Gospels, and they do not always agree.

Why Four Gospels?
Why four Gospels? Two related answers immediately present themselves. On the one hand, no one person is ever able to

capture the whole significance of any other person, and this is especially true for a person of Jesus' stature and originality. As helpful a portrait of Jesus as Luke provided his readers he was still incapable of capturing everything of importance. For this reason we may be thankful that we have not one but four portraits of Jesus.

On the other hand, different Christian communities, even in apostolic times, required their own account of Jesus' ministry and its significance, told in a manner especially suited to them. As we will see more fully in chapter four, the Gospels are *purposeful documents.* To use different language, we might say that in some ways the Gospels, like Paul's letters, are "occasional writings." That is, just as Paul wrote his first letter to the Christians at Corinth to address specific problems there (see, for example, 1 Cor 1:11; 5:1; 7:1), so each of the evangelists wrote his Gospel to address certain needs.[1] It is only natural, then, that the Gospel of John should have taken on a different flavor than the Gospel of Matthew; John had in mind a different readership.

In fact, many "gospels" were written in the first centuries of the church. Luke himself was aware of a number of attempts at telling the story of Jesus prior to his own (Lk 1:1). Hence, gospels (of some kind) were no doubt being circulated in the early decades of Christianity. We also know that the impetus toward writing gospels continued for several centuries. Some such attempts have been known in their entirety by biblical scholars for a long time; others, quoted by ancient writers, have been known only by name; still others have come to light only in relatively recent years among the archaeological finds at Nag Hammadi.

In all probability the gospels of this latter group (sometimes refered to as "apocryphal gospels") were written much later than those found in the New Testament. Their contents are sometimes highly entertaining and include both fantastic stories about Jesus and enigmatic, esoteric sayings allegedly uttered by Jesus.[2] As we know, however, only four Gospels—Matthew, Mark, Luke and John—gained widespread authoritative status. Perhaps the rise of other gospels, less grounded in history and more given to speculative interpretation, provided the impetus toward the recognition of our New Testament Gospels as authoritative accounts.

Still, even at that early date, some uneasiness was apparently felt over having multiple witnesses to Jesus' story. A certain tension resulted when different accounts were simply placed side by side. By way of solving this problem, the first "harmony of the Gospels" was created. Its author, Tatian, strove to distill the variant narratives of the four Gospels into a single, authoritative account. In the end, this did not prove satisfactory to the ancient church either.

The ancient solution to the problem of four Gospels is perhaps best seen in the titles given them. Originally, the Gospels would have circulated with no headings, and only as they were collected together were titles required. Translated straightforwardly, these writings were entitled, "According to Matthew," "According to Mark" and so on. The idea behind these designations is not simply that Matthew, Mark, Luke and John wrote these books. Rather, this "according to" implies a fundamental conformity to the one story—that is, the one gospel—that all four evangelists are telling. There is only one gospel, but it has been rendered by four different writers.[3] In giving these four books this title, then, the ancient church bore witness to the ultimate unity of their focus and subject, while at the same time allowing for diversity in the narration of the story.

Four Gospels: Shared Authority

What does this mean for our understanding of the Gospels today? Two things. First, we must be clear that in selecting all four Gospels and placing them side by side, the early church asserted, in effect, that no one Gospel is "better" or "more correct" than another. Of course, in acknowledging the active role of the ancient church in the canonization of the Gospels, we are not suggesting that this was merely a human enterprise. Quite the contrary, we believe that the Holy Spirit guided this whole process.[4]

What does it mean to suggest that all four Gospels are granted equal status? Fundamentally, it means that all four Gospels are equally valid witnesses to the one gospel, even though they do testify to that gospel in distinctive ways. Each must be allowed to stand on its own. Thus John's Gospel can never be regarded as the key for unlocking the message of the Gospel of Mark. Each Gospel retains its own integrity as a literary work. However, this also means that no one Gospel is adequate *on its own* as the authoritative witness to the gospel. Because they are told from different perspectives, they complement one another; they balance one another; each reveals a different aspect of the character of the one gospel—that is, of the significance of Jesus' life, death and resurrection. All four are needed, and no individual account can be singled out as the most faithful witness to Jesus' significance.

We can illustrate this last point with reference to one of the Beatitudes, given in two different forms in Matthew and Luke:

Blessed are the poor in spirit,

for theirs is the kingdom of heaven. (Mt 5:3)

Blessed are you who are poor,

for yours is the kingdom of God. (Lk 6:20)

Here we are not concerned that Matthew's version is given in the third person ("theirs") and Luke's in the second ("yours"), or that Matthew refers to the kingdom of *heaven,* while Luke writes of the kingdom of *God.* (In fact, "kingdom of heaven" and "kingdom of God" are synonymous expressions.)[5] The more substantial problem with these parallel verses centers on the apparent reference in Matthew's version to "the spiritually poor," as opposed to the apparent reference in Luke's to "the materially poor." Recognizing both Gospels as equally authoritative witnesses to the one gospel requires that we resist all efforts to emphasize or prefer one version over the other. We need to hear *both,* and we highlight one against the other only to our detriment.

Hence, while we appreciate and applaud the recovery by many evangelicals of the biblical truth concerning God's predisposition toward the oppressed—and thus our own responsibility on their behalf—we must call for an appreciation of the *whole* story. With good reason socially-aware evangelicals have turned their attention to the Gospel of Luke in an effort to ground their concerns in the essence of the gospel.[6] In many ways the Third Gospel is well suited to this endeavor, with its emphasis on Jesus as the Savior of all, even (or especially) of the disadvantaged. Luke, however, is only one of four Gospels; it is not the whole story. To neglect Matthew, Mark and John in any attempt to get to the heart of Jesus' message is to fly in the face of the reality that we have before us *a fourfold Gospel!* No one Gospel, then, is complete in itself as a testimony to the gospel.

Incidentally, when we take into account the significance of the term *poor* in the years before and after the earthly ministry of Jesus, we recognize no inherent contradiction between Matthew's and Luke's versions of this beatitude. Because of the social and political conditions under foreign rule during this period (which we will look at in the next chapter), faithfulness toward God might and often did entail material deprivation. That is, both expressions, "poor" (socioeconomic poverty) and "poor in spirit" (pious humility), would have embraced both religious and social dimensions of life. In reporting this saying of Jesus, then, Matthew and Luke are pointing to the same reality while emphasizing its different aspects.

The Gospel Message for Today
What other point of interpretation is suggested by the decision to include four Gospels in the New Testament? My second point is this: By choosing as Holy Scripture not a single "life of Jesus" (if, indeed, such were ever written) but four Gospels, the early Christians placed their stamp of approval on endeavors to couch the story of Jesus' ministry in forms and language designed to communicate its significance in new ways to different audiences. In a sense, what we have in the Gospels is essentially the same story told and retold again and again—never in quite the same way, always highlighting additional aspects of that story.

The same task is presented to us—and indeed to every successive generation of Christian believers. In order to re-present the gospel story we must immerse ourselves in the authoritative accounts we have so that we comprehend as fully as we can their message. But we must never stop at this point; this is only "step one." We must go on to ask how this message can best be communicated to ourselves, to our families, to our communities, to our cities and to our world. We must ask, what shape would a "gospel" take today? How would the narrative best be framed to witness to the one gospel in this new life situation?

Some have found that a simple retelling of the parables, with appropriate changes in their casts of characters, communicates powerfully today. In this case, the idea is to draw the modern reader or hearer into the story with the same intensity and sense of identification, empathy and shock experienced by the original audiences. There is also room for updating such stories as the birth narratives in order to communicate the surprise, even strangeness, of those accounts when communicated in the first-century world. Thus Joseph might be presented as an apprentice welder between jobs, the angels might appear to illegal aliens huddled around a fire, and so on—all set in the expanses of rural West Texas, far removed from the hubbub of important people and significant activity.[7]

Of course, these updated versions never replace our New Testament Gospels as *authoritative* witnesses to Jesus' message and its significance. They only assist the modern reader or listener in coming face to face in a life-changing encounter with that authoritative witness. Nevertheless, the character of the canonical Gospels themselves, as well as their selection to stand side by side in the New Testament, sets before us the imperative to retell the same story and reframe the same message for communication in our own day.

By suggesting that the Gospels tell and retell the same message of Jesus, we have implicitly raised the question whether our four Gospels share some literary relationship. Since this question is important for understanding the nature of the Gospels and their interpretation, we now turn to consider it.

Gospel Relationships

Which Gospel was written first? Did the other evangelists know this Gospel and make use of it in any way? In fact, it is highly likely that the first three Gospels, often referred to as the *Synoptic* Gospels, do share a literary relationship. Three factors support this judgment.

First, these three Gospels share a high degree of similarity in content. Of course, Matthew and Luke contain much more material than Mark, but it is surely noteworthy that only about twenty-four verses in Mark's Gospel are totally unique to Mark. That is, more then ninety-five percent of Mark's Gospel appears also in Matthew or Luke. This suggests that Mark either knew the First and Third Gospels and tried to combine them or that Matthew and Luke made use of Mark.

Second, these Gospels share the same general structure. All agree that Jesus' ministry was initiated by his baptism and temptation, that he carried on his public ministry in Galilee, and that Peter's confession at Caesarea Philippi was something of a watershed in Jesus' ministry. Finally, there is a large measure of coincidence in their parallel descriptions of the last journey up to Jerusalem, followed by Jesus' last meal, trial, crucifixion and the discovery of the empty tomb. Because of these similarities Matthew, Mark and Luke are regarded as *Synoptic* ("common-view") Gospels.

On their own these two observations suggest a literary relationship of some kind among the Synoptic Gospels, but a third factor is conclusive. There is a startling similarity in vocabulary and literary style in those many sections where the Synoptic Gospels coincide. That is, agreement extends far beyond content to embrace correspondence in style and wording. As an example of this phenomenon, consider the parallel stories of the cleansing of the leper in Matthew 8:2-4; Mark 1:40-44; Luke 5:12-14.

An inspection of these stories will indicate that the three correspond, often exactly, not only in their records of what Jesus said (which we might expect), but also in their descriptions of what took place. Gordon Fee of Regent College rightly draws

Matthew 8:2-4	Mark 1:40-44	Luke 5:12-14
And behold, a leper came to him and	And a leper came to him and on his	And behold, there came a man full of leprosy, and when he saw Jesus, he fell on
knelt before him, saying, "Lord, if you will, you can make me clean." And	knees, he begged him, saying to him, "Lord if you will, you can make me clean." And moved with compassion,	his face and begged him, saying, "Lord, if you will, you can make me clean." And
he stretched out his hand and touched him, saying, "I will; be clean." And immediately his leprosy was cleansed.	he stretched out his hand and touched him and said, "I will; be clean." And immediately his leprosy left him and he was cleansed. And he sent him away immediately with a warning,	he stretched out his hand and touched him, saying, "I will; be clean." And immediately his leprosy left him.
And Jesus said to him, "See that you tell no one; instead, go, show yourself to the priest and offer	and said to him "See that you tell no one anything; instead, go, show yourself to the priest and offer for your cleansing	And he ordered him to tell no one; "Instead, go, show yourself to the priest and offer for your cleansing
the gift which was commanded by Moses, as a proof to them."	that which was commanded by Moses, as a proof to them."	just as Moses commanded, as a proof to them."

attention to the remarkable verbal agreements in the Greek texts of these accounts (Greek being the language in which the Gospels were originally *written),* especially when it is noted that (1) the similarities are present despite the fact that the stories were originally spread *orally* in Aramaic; (2) Greek word order is extremely free, but similarities often extend even to word sequence; and (3) there is little likelihood that the three evangelists, writing in three different parts of the Roman Empire, would tell the same story using exactly the same words.[8]

Precisely these kinds of observations have led students of the Gospels to conclude that the Synoptic Gospels are related. But how? This debate, referred to as the Synoptic Problem, is long and intricate, and here we can only observe that most scholars

agree that Mark's Gospel was written first and was used inde-
pendently by Matthew and Luke as a primary source.[9] Can one
accept this assessment of the evidence *and* believe in the inspiration of the Scriptures? Certainly! Indeed, the use of sources
is explicitly noted by Luke (Lk 1:1-4). It was through this arrangement, we believe, that God chose to bring us the Synoptic
Gospels.

The discussion about John's relationship to the Synoptic Gospels is also a complex one. Let it suffice that the most probable
view is that the Fourth Gospel was not directly dependent on
Matthew, Mark or Luke.[10]

The remaining question is an important one: What differ-
ence does it make whether Luke and Matthew used the Gospel
of Mark? How does this knowledge assist us in interpreting the
Gospels? Realizing that the Synoptic Gospels are related in this
way encourages us to compare them in our study of individual
texts, and this allows us to note the distinctiveness of each in
communicating the gospel story. For this kind of study, a "Gospel parallel" or "Gospel synopsis," which presents the Gospels
in parallel columns, is an essential tool. (See, for example, Kurt
Aland, ed., *Synopsis of the Four Gospels* [United Bible Societies].)

We can illustrate the usefulness of this kind of study by looking at Jesus' prayer in Gethsemane (or, in Luke's narrative, on
the Mount of Olives).

Mark 14:36, 39, 41: "Abba, Father, . . . everything is possible
for you. Take this cup from me. Yet not what I will, but what
you will." . . . Once more he went away and prayed the same
thing. . . . Returning the third time . . . (NIV)

Matthew 26:39, 42, 44: "My Father, if it is possible, may this
cup be taken from me. Yet, not as I will, but as you will.". . .
"My Father, if it is not possible for this cup to be taken away
unless I drink it, may your will be done." . . .

So he left them and went away once more and prayed the
third time, saying the same thing. (NIV)

Luke 22:42: "Father, if you are willing, take this cup from
me; yet not my will, but yours be done." (NIV)

To these versions we may also add the parallel in John 12:27-

28: "Now my heart is troubled, and what shall I say? 'Father, save me from this hour'? No, it was for this very reason I came to this hour. Father, glorify your name!" (NIV).

Without attempting a lengthy commentary on these versions, we may venture a few observations:

1. Matthew explictly reports Jesus' third prayer, which can only be assumed in Mark; in this way he has smoothed out Mark's narrative.

2. Luke, on the other hand, has recorded only one instance of Jesus' prayer. By doing so, and by his choice of words, he has highlighted Jesus' firm resolve to carry out God's will even more than Mark's version does. This idea is even more firmly emphasized in John's version, where Jesus actually refuses to pray such a prayer.

3. Jesus' submission to the divine plan is further underscored by the way the prayer is phrased both in Matthew and Luke. Instead of requesting that the cup be removed, then adding the proviso regarding the will of God as in Mark, the request is in the form of a complex, conditional statement: "If it is your will, then . . ." This renders Jesus' readiness to obey much more apparent from the very outset of his prayer.

4. Finally, note the subtle changes in the wording of the prayer in Matthew and Luke when compared with Mark. In the First and Third Gospels there are clear echoes of the language of the Lord's Prayer as recorded in Matthew 6:10: "Your will be done." Similarly, in John's version, the phrase "Father, glorify your name" is parallel to the opening of the Lord's Prayer, "Hallowed be your name." Both ask that God bring his plan to fruition. With this language, we envision Jesus "practicing what he preaches," thus modeling for his disciples the submissive prayer he had taught them to pray.

While other observations could be made based on a comparison of these texts, this should adequately illustrate the point at hand. A comparison of parallel passages, particularly among the Synoptic Gospels, can be a tremendous aid toward coming to terms with the perspective and special concerns of each evangelist.

Conclusion

The problems raised by having four Gospels in our New Testament have plagued Christians, past and present. We have seen in this chapter, however, that the presence of a fourfold Gospel is actually a boon to modern Christians, not a bane. It gives us a much fuller perspective on the significance of Jesus' life, death and resurrection, and it compels us to search out ways of making that message relevant in our own contexts. Noting the literary relationships of the Gospels aids us in coming to terms with the concerns of each evangelist and provides us with an important basis from which to understand the Gospels.

3
Jesus in Historical Context

Jesus was a Jew. This fact may seem self-evident, and perhaps it is. In practice, however, it is a reality easily forgotten—especially among modern Christians in the West.[1] We tend to think of Jesus as a man of our own time—accustomed to our way of thinking, with our habits and concerns. As a result, we regularly overlook the significance of what Jesus was saying and doing *in his own time and among his own people.*

In bypassing the sometimes tedious exercise of placing Jesus within his own historical and cultural context, we make it impossible to grasp the significance of many of his actions and words. Without some background, for example, we could scarcely come to terms with the surprising character of Jesus' conversation with the Samaritan woman in John 4. Nor could we discern the importance of touching in Jesus' healing activities. Without some attention to historical context, we might with good reason wonder what was so incredible about Jesus' "eating with sinners." Indeed, as Kenneth Bailey has demonstrated, important points pertaining even to Jesus' teaching with parables are simply lost to us—unless we remember who Jesus was, when he lived, and the sort of people he addressed.[2] Jesus may have been the Incarnate Word, but he was also a first-century Jew. As such, he operated within *those* historical constraints. This was the price of the Incarnation. If we are to understand Jesus' message, we must take seriously *who he was in his own time.*

This "cultural distance" is only one reason we must take seriously Jesus' own historical and cultural context. In addition, we should recall that Christianity, like the Judaism from which it sprang, is a historical religion. That is, Christian faith focuses on a God who deals with real people in real history. Hence, the more we understand how God revealed himself in Jesus in real history, the greater will be our understanding of our Lord and our faith. For these reasons, we will in this chapter take on an important, if formidable, agenda: setting the historical and cultural backdrop for the entrance of Jesus onto the stage of Palestinian (and world!) history.[3]

To focus this whole problem, we may follow up our query about Jesus' "table fellowship." While studies of Jesus regularly focus on his words, no doubt his actions were an important part of his message as well. This is especially true for Luke, whose concern for "table scenes" has been the subject of several studies—but also most certainly for Mark and Matthew.[4] When we remember that the evangelists made choices about what to include and what to exclude from their narrative, we may rightly ask, Why was this so important?

This question is all the more pointed in that Jesus' table activities obviously appeared at one and the same time as *characteristic* of his ministry and *out of character* for the religious people of his day. On the one hand, we find a straightforward mission statement in which Jesus proclaims that *the reason for his coming* was to associate with sinners at the table (Mk 2:15-17).[5] To this we may add a number of texts which contribute to our impression that eating and drinking with sinners was typical of Jesus' behavior (see especially Mt 11:18-19; Lk 15:2; 19:7).

On the other hand, we find record in the Gospels that the ministers and seminary professors of Jesus' day were quite scandalized by Jesus' appalling behavior (above all, see Mt 11:19; Mk 2:16; Lk 15:2). The reasons for this are many and complex, and in a study of this nature we cannot hope to deal exhaustively with this stimulating issue. Nevertheless, we will see that even a sketchy understanding of the Judaism of Jesus' day places us in a better position to comprehend the significance of this and similar matters.

In what follows we will try to get a bird's-eye view of the historical terrain, and then center more pointedly on this one aspect of Jesus' ministry which both demonstrates the value of this sort of study and takes us to the heart of Jesus' uniqueness, self-understanding and mission.

Pre-Christian Judaism: An Overview

To lay a foundation for understanding Palestine in the days of Jesus, we will look at three or four key events during the period in question. The first takes us back to the opening of the sixth century B.C. (587): the destruction of Solomon's Temple by Nebuchadnezzar and the onset of the Babylonian Exile. Even though the official exile itself was to last a relatively short period of time (about fifty years) and probably involved only the upper class of the Jewish people, the consequences of these and subsequent events in the life of the people of God are immeasurable. Indeed, the return from the Exile marked a new era for Jewish religion.

What forces were at work here? Several could be enumerated, and all revolve around the apparent tension between the reality of destruction and exile on the one hand, and Israel's traditional faith on the other. For example, there was the pressing question regarding the throne. Did God not promise David an everlasting dynasty (see 2 Sam 7:13)? What of the land? Had God not bequeathed the land to Abraham and his seed (see Gen 22:17-18)? Yet now God's chosen people had neither a Son of David as king nor the ownership of the land deeded to them. They were faced with the prospect of existence under the overlordship of Babylon first, and then Persia, Greece and Rome.

Moreover, Israel's worship, which centered on the temple in

Jerusalem, was struck a mortal blow by the destruction of the temple itself. Still further, other gods—those of foreign vintage—threatened the monotheism which had distinguished Israel from its neighbors. The Old Testament scholar John Bright has hardly overstated his case when he comments, "With that, let us not mince it, the very status of Israel's God was thrown into question."[6] After the Exile, God's people and their faith could never again be the same.

If the Exile and foreign domination so markedly shaped the Judaism of Jesus' day, it is important to ask, What was happening to the faith of the Jews during this era? What pillars both rooted them in Old Testament faith and prepared them for an adequate reponse to these tumultuous times?[7]

Above all, we must take account of the Jewish attitude toward God and his covenant with his elect. Traditionally, Christians wanting to distinguish themselves from Judaism have drawn a sharp line between the Jewish emphasis on law and the Christian focus on grace. We now know that this is little more than a caricature of Judaism in Jesus' day, that the dominant theme of Jewish religion was not the law per se, but the covenant.[8] This should not surprise us, for the covenant is one of the most powerful and pervasive themes of Old Testament faith.

Behind the observance of the law stands the Exodus, which itself was branded onto the hearts of successive generations of the people of Israel. This was the ground of Israel's faith and her charter as a nation (see, for example, Ex 19:4-6).[9] The whole theology of the Exodus and covenant is the context in which we must come to terms with the later fascination with the law. *God's gracious act of deliverance demands human response!*

This point is clearly present in the way the giving of the Ten Commandments is reported in Exodus 20. In the preamble (vv. 1-2), God states who he is *in terms of his mighty act of deliverance.* Then, in the verses that follow (vv. 3-17) we read how God's people were to live in response to his graciousness. Keeping the law, therefore, was not to be an end in itself; rather, it was the proper response to a God who had previously acted on behalf of an oppressed people. Even among the later prophets, where the *language* of the covenant is not always at center stage, the *idea* of the covenant is never far from view. Indeed, their message might be summarized thus: You have broken my covenant; punishment is on the way (or has arrived already); return to me! Various first-century Jewish sects might nuance their view of the law in different ways, but all agreed on its centrality as a response to their God.

In discussing the centrality of covenant for Jewish religion we have already noticed the primacy of Israel's theology—that is, its understanding of the nature of God—for its faith and life. We might say that even more important for the faith of Israel was "the God behind the covenant." For the Jews, God was not an abstraction; nor was God known through speculation. This God was, instead, *the God of history,* and the relationship between God and his people was understood in terms of historical events. "To speak about God was to speak about the experiences of the Jewish nation throughout history."[10]

While God had revealed himself in the act of creation and in the created order (see, for example, Ps 19, 104), even more so he was known in the course of history. This was the history that was remembered and celebrated, and which formed the basis for Israel's understanding of who God is. Thus, at the inauguration of life in the new land, the land promised by God, the worshiper was told to recall God's action *in history* on behalf of his people:

> My father was a wandering Aramean, and he went down into Egypt with a few people and lived there and became a great nation, powerful and numerous. But the Egyptians mistreated us and made us suffer, putting us to hard labor. Then we cried out to the LORD, the God of our fathers, and the LORD heard our voice and saw our misery, toil and oppression. So the LORD brought us out of Egypt with a mighty hand and an outstretched arm, with great terror and with miraculous signs and wonders. He brought us to this place and gave us this land, a land flowing with milk and honey. (Deut 26:5-9 NIV)[11]

In spite of outward appearances—which might have been re-

garded as a contradiction of God's involvement in history—
Israel's faith remained surprisingly constant on this issue: The
God who had delivered Israel from the bondage of slavery
ruled history. In spite of the destruction of the temple and its
cult, in spite of the loss of self-rule, in spite of catastrophic
threats against Jewish faith, there remained the belief that God
was in control. He was working out his purpose.

The rebuilding of the temple after the Babylonian Exile and
the subsequent extensive speculation about the place of the
temple in the messianic kingdom testify to the continuing importance of the temple in the pre-Christian period.[12] However,
actual participation in temple worship in Jerusalem was limited,
even if the rank and file of the Jewish nation could hardly
forget the temple due to its taxation.

Following the Exile, the synagogue, not the temple, became
the most influential center of religious practice. The rise of the
synagogue was due in part to the reality of the dispersion of the
Jews, which necessitated some more localized worship center.
Moreover, the synagogue, with its focus on the explication of
the Hebrew Bible (our Old Testament) and its application to
everyday life, was better suited to the changing needs of the
people of God in intertestamental times. Still further, synagogues provided a forum in which the Hebrew Scriptures
could be translated into Aramaic, the common vernacular. The
proliferation of synagogues was also a boon for evangelistic
efforts among Gentiles—a point of no small consequence for
the rise of the early Christian mission.

One last pillar of faith worthy of mention at this early point
in our discussion of the shaping of Judaism in pre-Christian
times is the significance accorded the first five books of the
Hebrew Scriptures, the Torah. The weight given the Torah in
the intertestamental period will come as no surprise to students
of the Old Testament, for God's people drew their identity from
this section of the Hebrew Scriptures. The Torah tells the story
of Israel's election and deliverance; moreover, it explains the
conditions for living as God's chosen people. Hence, during
this time of turmoil, when other long-standing pillars of the

faith (for example, the monarchy, the land and the temple) were crumbling, the Torah was the underlying constant. As we will see shortly, pre-Christian Judaism related to the Torah in a variety of ways, but there can be no question that postexilic faith was more and more "a religion of the Book."

Some 250 years after the Babylonian Exile (that is, in 333 B.C.), long after Babylonian rule had given way to Persian, Palestine again changed hands, this time as a result of the successful campaigns of Alexander the Great. With Alexander came Hellenistic rule, and with it, "Hellenization" as a cultural process was instigated in Palestine.[13] Apparently, Alexander's vision was for a kind of "melting pot" among the various countries and peoples he had conquered—with the Hellenistic or Greek element serving as the common denominator for every people.

Though Alexander died only a decade after his conquest of Palestine, and his political successors lacked his ability to maintain political unity, the spread of Greek culture was not to be deterred. Hellenization constituted no small problem for the people of Israel. From the time of their charter as a nation, they had been called to maintain their uniqueness; they were not to adopt the ways of the peoples around them (see, for example, Deut 18:9-22). New developments, however, brought on by the influx of Hellenistic (=alien) ideas and ways, threatened Jewish separateness. With Hellenization came changes at every strata of society—trade and commerce, education and literature, the official adoption of the Greek language, and the pressures of religious pluralism.

Palestine occupied no enviable position in the period after Alexander's death, situated as it was between the empires of two of his generals—the Ptolemaic dynasty in Egypt and the Seleucid in the region of Syria. After approximately 100 years of oscillating between these two military powers, control of Palestine finally fell to the Seleucids at the turn of the second century B.C. Whatever struggles the Jewish people may have known from the beginnings of Hellenization some 135 years earlier pale into insignificance when compared with the unrest experienced under Seleucid reign in this new period. Of special importance to our brief survey of pre-Christian Judaism is the rise to power of Antiochus IV (Epiphanes) in 175 B.C.

Long before Antiochus Ephiphanes assumed the throne, the Hellenization of Palestinian culture had begun. However, what had been taking place gradually, almost naturally, now began to happen with new intensity, even force. And while before there had been no concerted effort to do away with "the laws of the fathers," in 167 B.C. Antiochus Epiphanes aggressively moved against the practice of the Jewish religion. As is clear from the apocryphal books of the Maccabees, Antiochus instigated a program where Jews were forced to participate in the pagan cult. Circumcision was outlawed, but the real litmus test for determining loyalty was the eating of pork. Those who refused faced painful execution.

There can be no doubt that these circumstances contributed significantly to the rise of a new "martyrological view of death" among the Jews. That is, death became more than "the end of life"—as it appears so often in the Old Testament—and instead was viewed as a heroic way to testify to the faith.[14] In fact, the witness of these early Jewish martyrs was regarded by some early Christians as worthy of emulation (see Heb 11:35-40).

Especially during this period, between the conquest of Palestine by Alexander and the first century A.D., the Jewish understanding of the oneness of God came under attack. It is impossible to understand the nature of Jewish faith in pre-Christian times (and the nature of anti-Christian polemic among Jews in later times) without realizing the tenacity with which it clung to its monotheism. Already, the Ten Commandments began with the admonition, "You shall have no other gods before me." And in the time of Jesus, the central confession of faith, known as the *shema*—"The LORD our God is one LORD" (Deut 6:4 NIV mg; see Deut 11:13-21; Num 15:37-41)—was to be recited twice daily.[15] Thus, while Greek and Roman religions were quite capable of accommodating additional deities—including the present reigning monarch—Judaism could scarcely have entertained any such notion.

The severity of the new king's policies sparked a rebellion against foreign intrusion into Jewish life. Led by the Maccabean family, this revolt enjoyed a measure of success: Jewish self-rule for a period of about 80 years, up to the Roman invasion of Palestine by Pompey in 63 B.C. Despite the religious freedom under self-rule, the process of Hellenization did not cease, and the whole period was marked by rampant internal strife. Even though the Jews were allowed a large degree of religious freedom under Roman overlordship, it did not bring immediate peace. In fact, it was not until A.D. 73, three years after the fall of Jerusalem, that the last Jewish resistance was squelched at Masada.[16]

During the whole period we have surveyed, we can trace the rise of a vitally important religious perspective, a perspective deeply embedded in the realities of postexilic faith. This development we call apocalyptic, from the Greek term for "revelation."[17] Apocalyptic arose as an attempt to answer the fundamental questions that present, historical reality raised against Israel's faith. As Paul D. Hanson has suggested, "The ancient Jewish apocalyptic writings grew out of the courage to stare into the abyss on the edge of which an entire civilization tottered, and a willingness to describe what the fantasy of faith enabled the human eye to glimpse beyond tragedy."[18]

With this new way of viewing reality, Israel found a new openness to God's *overarching plan;* pressure, then, was removed from explaining present travesty only in terms of the present. Additionally, emphasis fell on God's radical intervention at the end: *then* he would bring justice—salvation for God's chosen, judgment for their enemies. In the rise of apocalyptic, a hopeless people found new hope, focusing anew on the sovereign God whose deliverance would certainly come. Literarily, emphasis fell on unfolding hidden meanings in prophetic texts and contemporary visions. Thus, for example, in the apocryphal book of 2 Esdras, the apocalyptist tells how the Lord explained to him the fuller meaning of a vision given to Daniel, for "it was not explained to him as I now explain or have explained it to you" (12:10-12).

The relevance of these considerations for studying Jesus and the Gospels can easily be seen by looking at two or three brief examples. First, the importance of apocalyptic for Jesus and early Christianity should never be underestimated.[19] Mark 13 and its parallels in Matthew and Luke are pointedly apocalyptic in focus and format, and major aspects of Jesus' message were apocalyptic in orientation. Of course, in proclaiming the *presence* of the kingdom of God, Jesus instigated a significant shift in apocalyptic eschatology.[20] Again, the importance Jesus vested in the idea of covenant is pinpointed in the Last Supper accounts (Mk 26:26-29; Mk 14:22-25; Lk 22:15-20; 1 Cor 11:23-25). And one of the recurring motifs at the cutting edge of Jesus-Jewish relations was the law—its enduring authority and proper application to contemporary life. We will look briefly now at the diversity of practice in Jewish religion at the time of Jesus.

Sects in First-Century Judaism

We must be careful to recognize that there was not one monolithic response among Jews to the historical developments after the Exile. Indeed, modern interpreters sorely miss the mark by suggesting that at the time of Jesus there was only one brand of Judaism. In the same way that Christians today wander from the truth when making statements about "what all Roman Catholics believe" or "what all United Methodists believe," we can scarcely refer to "what all Jews believed" at the time of Jesus with any accuracy. To be sure, there were common features that held the various Jewish sects within the boundaries of Judaism, but on many points their diversity was remarkable. I propose to outline four Jewish sects by focusing above all on the response of each to Hellenization and (where appropriate) the attitudes of each to the temple and the Torah.[21]

1. The Pharisees. Pharisaism was essentially a lay movement which took seriously the obligation laid upon Israel to be a holy nation. For Pharisees, this entailed an emphasis on maintaining purity in everyday life—so that what was historically expected in terms of holiness *within* the temple now became normative *outside* the temple. Hence, the temple did not occupy center stage in Pharisaism. Instead, the Torah was spotlighted. In fact, the move among Pharisees was toward spelling out the implications of the law so that it was absolutely relevant for every aspect of life. Not surprisingly, then, the synagogue had great significance for the Pharisee. Because personal holiness could be practiced in everyday life, Pharisaism adopted a passive tolerance of Hellenization.

2. *The Sadducees.* The Sadducees, on the other hand, were apparently quite friendly toward the influx of Hellenistic culture. Inasmuch as they represented the aristocracy of Jewish society, they had most to gain from changes in educational, economic and political spheres. Sadducees held a much more conservative attitude toward the law, believing that the priestly laws of the Torah were limited to the priests and the goings-on in the temple. The temple and its priesthood, then, constituted the focal point of Israel's holiness.

The Pharisaic movement developed in opposition to this way of thinking, and not surprisingly the Sadducees refused to adopt the sometimes ingenious methods of the Pharisees (and other groups) for applying the biblical message in the contemporary setting. To give one interesting example, unlike the Pharisees, the Sadducees rejected the notion of a resurrection, for they were unable to locate that idea in the Torah.[22] Hence, Pharisaism was more a "party for the people," but the real power brokers of first-century Palestine were the Sadducees.

3. *The Essenes.* The discovery between 1947 and 1956 of the Dead Sea Scrolls at Qumran has greatly increased our understanding of the diversity within Judaism at the time of Jesus. While the Essenes were not to be found exclusively at Qumran, the remains of this monasticlike community give us our best information about the sect. At the heart of the Qumranic expression of Judaism is the sectarian stance over against Judaism as a whole as impure, tainted by Hellenistic influence. Understandably, then, the Essenes rejected temple worship per se and in fact physically removed themselves from participation in its worship. In its place they substituted their own community, which they regarded as the eschatological temple. Theirs was

a fundamentally, even fanatically, eschatological community—separate unto God, his remnant and covenant people, ready for the Last Battle against the Kingdom of Darkness.

4. The Zealots. The Zealots, too, reacted strongly against Hellenism. However, instead of withdrawing from Palestinian life like the Qumran sectarians, their response was one of militant defiance. Perhaps holding in high regard the earlier Judas Maccabeus (who led the Maccabean revolt), the Zealots directed their efforts toward purging Palestine from alien influence and overlordship.

These, then, were the four main parties of first-century Judaism. Their positions, emphases, practices and ideologies provide much of the context for understanding the nature of Jesus' message and the impact he would have had in his own setting. We have now set the historical stage for beginning to look more closely at the Gospels themselves. However, before departing this background survey, we must return to the questions raised at the beginning of this chapter concerning the significance of Jesus' relationship with "sinners," and especially his habits of table fellowship. Here we will see in one case how a knowledge of Jesus' historical context aids our appreciation of his mission.

Jesus and "Sinners" at the Table

In coming to terms with the extraordinary character of Jesus' involvement at the table with sinners, we need to treat two interrelated questions—the first having to do with why the leaders of the Jews reacted so negatively toward this aspect of Jesus' ministry, the second having to do with the significance of this practice in the Gospels.

In Mark 2:16 we gain the impression that the Pharisees and teachers of the Law advised Jesus' disciples to leave his company; after all, he ate with tax collectors and sinners! Similarly, in Luke's Gospel, first the Pharisees and teachers of the Law (15:2), then "all the people" (19:7) expressed dismay at Jesus' eating and drinking with sinners. Why this reaction? What was so objectionable about this behavior?

At the root of the Jewish response to Jesus lay the age-old way in which boundaries were drawn in Old Testament and Jewish faith, especially between what was clean and unclean.[23]

More particularly, however, we must come to terms with how radically sharing a meal in our contemporary Western culture differs in significance from eating together in ancient Judaism. For them, though often not for us, *table fellowship was the closest form of intimacy*. To share a meal together involved persons in the most intimate of social bonds—and so the righteous should not share a table with sinners (Ps 1:1). The depth of this way of thinking is perhaps nowhere suggested more strongly than in Psalm 41:9, where betrayal by a table intimate is regarded as the worst tragedy imaginable (Jn 13:18). This explains the preoccupation with the placing of table guests in Luke 14:7-14 (see Mk 10:35-45, especially v. 37) and the question of invitations in the parable of the great banquet (Lk 14:15-24; see also 14:12-14).

More than the social order was at stake with table fellowship, however, for eating together involved more than encounters between men and women. Meals were significantly *religious occasions*, for meals were partaken in the presence of the Lord God. The meal at the making of the covenant in Sinai was an eating and drinking in the presence of God at which time the leaders of the Israelites "beheld God" (Ex 24:8-11). In reading the book of Deuteronomy we discover that God has not only chosen his people, but has also chosen their place of habitation, and has called them to celebrate before him with food and drink (see, for example, Deut 12:5-7, 17-18; 14:23, 26; 27:7). He prepares a table (Ps 23:5) and issues the invitation to feast (Prov 9:1-6).[24]

Hence, meals were not to be taken for granted. They were to be prepared for, as with the Pharisees, by ritual washings (Mk 7:3-4), and never should Jews be found at the same table with Gentiles (see Gal 2:11-13!). Indeed, at Qumran, only persons who had been properly initiated were welcome at the common table, and even then there were proper "table manners" to be observed.

Enter Jesus! His eating and drinking seemed anything but

regulated. Thus his decision to eat with Zacchaeus was all too spontaneous (Lk 19:1-10). He obviously remained open to sharing food and drink with *anyone*. Not only that, he *enjoyed* this seemingly frivolous, worldly behavior (see Mt 11:18-19)! No wonder many of his contemporaries were scandalized by his "unholiness," his failure to appreciate and follow long-standing social and religious conventions.

However, we may wonder if early Christians did not see more in Jesus' table manners than his mere flouting of these practices. Was there not something deeper, richer about this aspect of Jesus' life which impressed itself upon those early disciples? What was the significance of Jesus' table fellowship with sinners?

At the most fundamental level, we must point to *Jesus' behavior as profoundly inclusive.* The message embodied in this activity was one of acceptance and graciousness—a message which later blossomed literarily in a text like Galatians 3:28: "There is neither Jew nor Greek, slave nor free, male nor female, for you are all one in Christ Jesus" (NIV). That is, the old categories no longer have meaning, the dividing walls are destroyed (Eph 2:14-18).

What is more, we see that in sharing the table with sinners, *Jesus mediated to them the salvation of God.* In Mark's account, Jesus involved himself with sinners not in order to become like them, but precisely to become their physician (2:15-17). Similarly, at the close of his encounter with Zacchaeus, Jesus asserted that "salvation has come to this house today" (Lk 19:9). For such encounters as this the Son of Man came (Lk 19:10).

Finally, and more significant in terms of drawing out the meaning of Jesus' table fellowship with sinners in terms of widely held beliefs in pre-Christian Judaism, we find that table encounters with Jesus were recognized as *an anticipation and foretaste of the heavenly banquet.* In this regard, immediate attention may be drawn to Luke 14:15, where a person sharing a meal with Jesus remarked, "Blessed is the man who will eat at the feast in the kingdom of God" (NIV). Embodied in this statement is a common anticipation which pictured the kingdom of

God in banquet terms (see Is 25:6-9; 32:12; 55:1-2; 65:13; Rev 19:17).[25]

The following verses (Lk 14:16-24) provide what would certainly have been regarded as a surprising guest list: the poor, the crippled, the blind and the lame—all from within Judaism (that is, from within "the city")—*and* Gentiles (that is, those from the highways and hedges with no previous knowledge of the master of the house). According to this parable the old view of who will be blessed in the kingdom must be radically transformed. Not the Jewish "guest list" (those who "deserve" to sit at the banquet), but Jesus' (those who respond to unbelievable grace) must be regarded as normative! That is, *Jesus' table fellowship prefigures the kingdom-feast* and, in fact, proclaimed that the kingdom had come in Jesus' activity.

Interestingly, the Lord's Prayer embraces this same eschatological edge with regard to eating. We pray, "Give us this day our daily bread"—and this is certainly correct (Mt 6:11; Lk 11:3). However, the sense intended by Jesus may well have been "give us this day the bread for *that* day" or "give us today *tomorrow's* bread."[26] In either case, we affirm that daily provision comes from God, but in the latter we are also taking hold of an explicitly eschatological dimension to his provision. Here, we are praying for earthly bread to meet daily need *and* for the bread of the kingdom which will feed God's people in eternity and which we already share in anticipation.

Finally, we may ask, Why were Jesus' table manners so important to the evangelists, and especially to Luke? No doubt, at one level these writers were merely being faithful in their representation of Jesus' behavior. In addition, we know from Acts 15 and Galatians 2 (to mention only two texts) that the problem of Jew-Gentile relations loomed large for the early church. In presenting this portrait of Jesus, the evangelists could have been appealing to Jesus' own example in order to preach a barrier-breaking message to their readers.

Conclusion

In this chapter I have argued that a more full and proper

understanding of the message of the Gospels is available to us by setting their narrated events in their own historical context. First-century Palestine, not the twentieth-century West, was the stage on which Jesus carried out his ministry, and our reading of the Gospels must never neglect this reality. At the same time, we must be cautious of tendencies in our own day to see the Judaism of Jesus' day as a single, monolithic movement. In this there is a broad similarity to contemporary history: religious movements are not easily herded down a narrow path, nor do they take a consistently homogeneous form. (One way to remind ourselves of this fact is to recall that Christianity itself originated as a Jewish sect!) As we have seen in the case of Jesus' table fellowship with sinners, drawing on Old Testament and intertestamental background and taking into account the socioreligious context of Jesus' day places us in a better position to see the significance of who he was and what he was about.

PART II
The Nature of the Gospels

4
The Gospels
as
Good News

What is a *Gospel?* For most readers of the Bible today, this hardly seems an appropriate or meaningful question.[1] We have grown accustomed to referring to the first four books of our New Testament by this name. For us, a Gospel is a book which narrates something about Jesus' life—focusing especially on his public ministry, death and the empty tomb. Because of our familiarity with this terminology, we might be surprised to discover that first-century Christians probably knew no such usage. They may well have been shocked to hear these written accounts of Jesus' career called Gospels.

Gospel in the Ancient World
Not that men and women of the ancient world were unfamiliar with the word *gospel* itself.[2] In the Greek version of the Old Testament, written around the third century B.C., the noun *euangelion* is found several times. Even in those contexts where it signifies "good news" (see, for example, 2 Sam 4:10; 18:22), however, it carries no explicitly religious nuance. On the other hand, the verb *euangelizomai*, "to preach the good news," is related to the proclamation of salvation in Isaiah 52:7:

How beautiful on the mountains
   are the feet of those who bring good news,
who proclaim peace,
   who bring good tidings,
   who proclaim salvation,
who say to Zion,
   "Your God reigns!" (NIV)
Similarly, in Isaiah 61:1 the good news is redemptive in content:
   The Spirit of the Sovereign LORD is on me,
      because the LORD has anointed me
      to preach good news to the poor. (NIV)
The gospel then is something to be preached; it is the message
of God's salvation proclaimed. Recognizing the religious connotations of this "good news" is one thing, but using that designation for a written work is quite another!

In the Hellenistic world, the term *gospel* or *good news* was most
prominently associated with the announcement of victory in
battle. Of special significance for us is a further use of the term
in this ancient culture. *Gospel* was connected with the worship
of the emperor (that is, the imperial cult) as a term for describing the ruler's oracles and activities. In fact, it has been suggested that the early church, making headway in a Hellenistic environment, adopted the term *gospel* precisely because it had
these connotations. In this way, Christians contrasted the "gospel of Jesus" with the "gospel of the emperor"—thus declaring
their loyalty to the Risen Lord.

Gospel in Mark
Justin, an early church leader who died about 165, was the first
to refer to the writings of the New Testament evangelists as
"Gospels." Nevertheless, the noun is found several times already in the Gospel of Mark. In Mark 8:35 ("for whoever would
save his life will lose it, but whoever loses his life for my sake
and the gospel's will save it"), a close relationship is drawn
between Jesus and the gospel. The two, "gospel" and "Jesus,"
appear in parallel. The impression we get is that a commitment
to one is understood as a commitment to the other (see also Mk

10:29). Moreover, in Mark's usage the gospel appears as something objective, something with content. Similarly, we read in Mark 13:10 that "the gospel must be preached to all nations" (see further Mk 1:14-15; 14:9).

The other outstanding use of *gospel* in Mark is in the evangelist's opening verse: "the beginning of the gospel of Jesus Christ, the Son of God" (1:1). We will take up this introductory text again in the next chapter; here we can note that Mark appears to be telling his readers that what follows is the "gospel." That is, the story he is about to relate is a verbal statement of the gospel.[3]

The Gospel as Good News

We might therefore regard the Gospel of Mark—and with it, the other Gospels—as *sermons.* Better yet, they might be called "preachings." They employ the story of Jesus in such a way as to preach the good news of Jesus. In his study *Mark: The Gospel as Story,* Ernest Best outlines some useful points for making sense of the Gospels when understood as preachings.[4]

First, as a preaching, each Gospel is related to a particular situation. Their evangelist-authors did not write the Gospels in order that they might be placed in the New Testament as authoritative, timeless witnesses to God's redemptive work in the life of Jesus of Nazareth. Indeed, when the Gospels were written there was no New Testament! Rather, the four Gospels were directed at particular people, living in particular circumstances. They were first designed to apply the gospel message to particular needs. By telling the story of Jesus' mission in a certain way, each evangelist sought to proclaim a vital word from God to his audience.

Second, by naming the Gospels "preachings," we understand that God is speaking through each of them. They constitute more than an interesting form of literature, more than a fascinating tale of a man who lived and died hundreds of years ago. Through Jesus' words and actions as recorded in the Gospels the Risen Lord lives again and his life speaks authoritatively to a new generation of men and women. Through these writings the evangelists continue to preach the gospel!

Third, as a "preaching," each Gospel is a unique combination of history and theology. Event and interpretation are welded together in such a way that the Jesus story is told and the reader is confronted with a particular and authoritative message. This aspect of the Gospels as "preachings" is vitally important to our reading them, but it is also one of the most debated points in the study of the Gospels today. For this reason it will be necessary to discuss this further.

New Testament Scholars: Raising Doubts?

Many Christians today—whether ordained or not—share a basic distrust of New Testament scholarship. Attempts to deny the resurrection, the historical character of the Gospels, or the possibility of knowing anything about Jesus of Nazareth are regularly paraded before us in newspapers and national magazines. What is particularly distressing about these reports of skepticism is that they often stem from *within* the church community.

Recently, for example, a self-appointed "Jesus Seminar," made up of a number of respected scholars, has taken upon itself the task of determining which of the words of Jesus in the Gospels are really authentic, which deserve to be printed in red in our red-letter editions. By means of a series of ballots its members have begun categorizing the sayings of Jesus according to the probability of their genuineness. No wonder critical scholarship on the Gospels has often been held at arm's length!

Can we trust the Gospels? Have recent developments in New Testament scholarship eroded our ability to believe what we read in the Gospels? In the two chapters that follow we will look more closely at the historical and theological character of the Gospels. Here I want to present an initial and introductory answer to this pressing question by focusing on two extreme viewpoints.

The Gospels: Lives of Jesus?

Throughout the church today Christians are often tempted to read the Gospels as though their primary function were merely to tell us precisely what Jesus said and did. Emphasis is placed on the exact words Jesus spoke and on the precise ordering of events. No doubt this point of view largely stems from rather modern aspirations among professional historians to be totally objective and to tell "what really happened." Having arisen in the guild of historians in the nineteenth and twentieth centuries, such emphases have penetrated nonprofessional spheres and have significantly influenced the way the reading public trusts the printed word. As a result we are often asked to regard first-century writings as though they were authoritative biographies written to our standards for "objective" historiography.

This is not a problem only for readers of the Gospels in this generation, however. The terrain of Gospel research since the turn of the nineteenth century is littered with scores of efforts at producing from the Gospels a coherent, historical portrait of Jesus' life. In a pointed and devastating critique of those earlier efforts, Albert Schweitzer, the New Testament scholar turned medical missionary, demonstrated that readers often find only what they are looking for in the Gospels.[5]

New Testament research suggests that the evangelists—Matthew, Mark, Luke and John—never intended to write Jesus' biography, in the modern sense of the word.[6] That is, they were concerned neither to write a "life of Jesus," as a modern historian would go about such a task, nor to provide raw material for such a record. In part, however, this conclusion is a result of our increasing recognition that a totally objective history can never really be written. It is simply impossible to tell "what actually happened." Every attempt to relate a human story involves a selection of events from the great reservoir of the raw material of which history is made. And behind the selection of material is a conviction about what is significant, what needs to be told. In addition, we have come to realize that what we in the twentieth century might regard as important was not necessarily what first-century Christians thought important.

We may illustrate this from the Gospels fairly easily. First is the obvious *problem of chronology* in the Gospel records. Here we are not concerned with any supposed discrepancies between the Gospels; rather, we are recognizing a surprising lack of information if the Gospels were intended to tell the story of Jesus' life. When was Jesus born? At what age did he begin his ministry? What was the duration of his public ministry? In what year was he crucified? We would expect any biography written today to provide such important details. Yet, without the Gospel of Luke we would have almost nothing to say to such queries. Even with the Third Gospel, answers to such (as we might suppose) major points come only after meticulous detective work combined with a large dose of speculation.

Consider the date of Jesus' birth. The hazards of pinpointing even such a momentous event as this are manifest in a sixth-century attempt to do so. Charged with the task of preparing a standard calendar for the Christian church in the West, Dionysius Exiguus named as year A.D. 1 the 754th year from the foundation of Rome. This, he calculated, was the year of Christ's incarnation. Since then, however, it has become clear that the latest date for Herod's death was the year 750 by the old reckoning—or 4 B.C. by the new. Because Jesus' birth is dated both by Matthew and Luke as having taken place prior to Herod's death (Mt 2:1; Lk 1:5), Dionysius must have missed the date of Jesus' birth by at least 4 years! According to Matthew and Luke, then, the latest year for Jesus' birth is 4 B.C.

Luke 2:1-2 appears to offer a more precise time reference: "In those days Caesar Augustus issued a decree that a census should be taken of the entire Roman world. (This was the first census that took place while Quirinius was governor of Syria)" [NIV]. However, this text provides no easy escape from our dilemma, for Quirinius was governor *after* the death of Herod and conducted his census in A.D. 6-7. Numerous attempts at overcoming this obstacle have been made—including the theory that Quirinius held an earlier governorship or some other extraordinary command alongside the regular governor of Syria—but none have won widespread support.[7]

In the case of Matthew and Luke, then, it appears that the ruling concerns were not when Jesus was born, or even *that* he was born, but why. These two evangelists devoted their literary

energies to drawing out *the significance* of this event. Luke's
primary motivation for including such references, it seems, was
to fix the significance of the birth of Jesus in the context of
world history. For him this was not the mere birth of a baby
in a Roman backwoods. Rather, this was an event destined to
change the course of history.

Problems of dating in the Gospel are not restricted to the
time of Jesus' birth. According to Luke 3:23, Jesus was "about
thirty years old when he began his ministry," but there is no
hard evidence for determining its duration. A reading of Mark's
Gospel might leave one with the impression that only a few
months elapsed from the time of Jesus' baptism to his crucifixion. John, on the other hand, narrated Jesus' participation in
no less than two Passover celebrations (2:13; 11:55; see also
6:4), and this suggests a two- or three-year span of time. We can
conclude only that we have no direct testimony that would lead
us to a certain conclusion and that the evangelists were obviously more interested in the importance and meaning of Jesus' ministry than in its length.

Similarly, we are not told the year of Jesus' crucifixion, and
it can be established as either A.D. 30 or 33 only by means of
astronomical study.

Are we denying the historical value of the Gospels? Are we
suggesting that the evangelists acted irresponsibly? Not at all!
We are merely pointing out that our concerns were not theirs,
that writing emphases have changed over the past two millen-
nia, and that we are mistaken when we read the Gospels as
though they were modern biographies or history textbooks. We
can support this assertion with other kinds of evidence.

We may refer also to the *sequence of events* as they are narrated
in the Gospels. Of course, when we consider the Gospels in
their broadest outline there is little variation. The beginning of
Jesus' public ministry is marked by his baptism by John, the
triumphal entry precedes his passion and so on. On closer
examination, however, we see that on matters of order the
Gospels can follow somewhat divergent paths. Consider, for
example, the order of the following events:[8]

	Matthew	Mark	Luke
Cleansing of the Leper	8:1-4	1:40-45	5:12-16
The Centurion of Capernaum	8:5-13	—	7:1-10
The Widow's Son at Nain	—	—	7:11-17
The Healing of Peter's Mother-in-Law	8:14-15	1:29-31	4:38-39
The Sick Healed at Evening	8:16-17	1:32-34	4:40-41
On Following Jesus	8:18-22	—	9:57-62
Stilling the Storm	8:23-27	4:35-41	8:22-25
The Gadarene Demoniac	8:28-34	5:1-20	8:26-39
The Healing of the Paralytic	9:1-8	2:1-12	5:17-26

This comparison shows considerable variation in the order in which the first three Gospels present the same events. Not only are the respective sequences different, but Matthew actually closely associates events which both Mark and Luke scatter over several chapters. What does this demonstrate? Only that the evangelists never intended to give us a precise, chronological account of Jesus' ministry. Moreover, the fact that not all the Gospels relate the same events suggests that the evangelists were also not interested in telling us everything that happened. This should not surprise us, though, for Luke and John clearly tell us that they were selective in their use of the stories about Jesus known to them (Lk 1:1-4; Jn 20:30; 21:25).

One interesting point of divergence in narrated order is the cleansing of the temple. Matthew, Mark and Luke all record this incident during Jesus' final ministry in Jerusalem, toward the end of their Gospels (Mt 21:12-13; Mk 11:15-19; Lk 19:45-46). John, on the other hand, narrates the cleansing of the temple at the very beginning of Jesus' ministry (Jn 2:13-17).

We can be certain that an event of this kind did take place during Jesus' public ministry, but when? Some might insist that John and the other Gospel writers are all correct, that there were, in fact, *two* temple-cleansings—one at the beginning, the other at the close of Jesus' ministry. However, having discovered that the Gospel writers never intended to give a precise chronology of Jesus' activity, we need no longer insist on a strict harmonizing of the accounts.

On the contrary, what is clear is that an intense confrontation, which this event represents, did take place in Jesus' ministry. In the first three Gospels, it serves as the last straw, driving the Jewish opposition to take decisive steps against Jesus. John, on the other hand, deemed it important to narrate it earlier rather than later.[9] As an historian, John narrated an historical event—the cleansing of the temple. As an evangelist and theologian, he placed that event early on in Jesus' public ministry. In this way, he uses the story to dramatize the opposition between Jesus and Jewish religion and to tell his readers from the beginning that this man Jesus is now the crucified-and-raised Lord who has replaced the temple.

Again, then, we see that the Gospel writers tell the story of Jesus *as Gospel writers,* and not as so-called objective historians or biographers.

Finally, we may notice that on *matters of detail* the evangelists reveal that they are not strictly interested in merely recounting a straightforward narrative of factual events. For example, what were Jesus' last words at his crucifixion? The Gospels give us three or four options:

"Eli, Eli, lama sabachthani?"—that is, "My God, my God, why have you forsaken me?" (Mt 27:46)

"Eloi, Eloi, lama sabachthani?"—which means, "My God, my God, why have you forsaken me?" (Mk 15:34)

"Father, into your hands I commit my spirit!" (Lk 23:46)

"It is finished!" (Jn 19:30)

Of course, there is no substantial difference between Matthew and Mark, but interestingly Matthew's "Eli, Eli" suggests Jesus spoke these words in Hebrew, while Mark's "Eloi, Eloi" suggests he spoke in Aramaic. Both mean "My God, my God," but the different versions raise the question of which most accurately represents the historical event.

As for the differences between Matthew-Mark, Luke and John, traditionally the accounts have been harmonized, and we have understood that Jesus said all three from the cross, one after the other. (Note the number of pre-Easter sermon series on "The Seven Last Words of Jesus.") This may well be. Even so, it raises the question why, for example, Luke did not record the quotation from Psalm 22:1 as we read in Mark. And why did John not include the citation from Psalm 31:5 found in Luke? Obviously, the Gospels do not intend to provide us with an on-the-spot, verbatim report of every word said and every deed done.

What are we to conclude from these observations? We have seen that the Gospels are not mere archives of Jesus' life, nor even of his public ministry. We do not find in their pages data from which to construct a "life of Jesus," nor do we find there the fruit of any attempt to write Jesus' biography from the perspective of an uninterested observer. We should not imagine, then, that the evangelists intended to tell us everything that happened, exactly as it happened. In emphasizing this point, New Testament scholars have helped the modern church immeasurably by suggesting what we may and may not expect the Gospels to say and do. Have New Testament scholars not gone too far in emphasizing this point, however?

The Gospels: Early Church Creations?

Just short of a century ago, New Testament scholars began to raise pointed questions about the whole endeavor of constructing a "life of Jesus." They began to regard the Gospels as books "written from faith to faith" and thus governed almost exclusively by theological interests.

In the first half of the twentieth century a new approach to Gospels study, form criticism, rose in influence. Form criticism, as it was widely practiced at that time, was based on the assumption that the stories and sayings of Jesus floated as independent traditions in the earliest years of Christianity. Moreover, as the church had need, either for evangelistic preaching or community life, it was quite capable of reforming or even creating sayings of and stories about Jesus.

Others argued that in an effort to dramatize Jesus' life, miraculous stories and profound sayings were borrowed from other religions by early Christians, who recast them with Jesus as the central figure. The evangelists, it was said, simply collected these individual early church traditions and set them down in written form.[10] How far this seems from efforts at writing a biography of the real historical Jesus!

While some of the assumptions about the nonhistorical character of the Gospels live on, the role of the Gospel writers has been rethought in recent times. Many students of the New Testament now emphasize the creative rather than custodial role of the evangelists. That is, the evangelists are largely noted not for their faithfulness to the tradition about Jesus, but for their creative role in telling the story of Jesus. Consequently, it is not unusual to hear someone speak about "Matthew's Jesus" as opposed to, say, "John's Jesus."

Of course, there is some truth to this way of viewing things, for we cannot deny that the four Gospel writers relate their narratives from their own perspectives. After all, every person, when recounting an event, colors the story to some degree by the way she or he tells it. For example, Matthew and Luke present much more of the content of Jesus' teaching than Mark, and John devotes a much larger percentage of his Gospel to Jesus' last week. Such decisions on the part of the evangelists as to what to include or exclude tell us something about their interests, what they considered important.

> As would any responsible preacher or pastor, the Gospel writers sought not only to *preserve* the gospel . . . but to *interpret* it so as to address the issues vital to the life and faith of the church. To the extent that they told the stories of Jesus so as to preserve and proclaim the gospel, we may expect them to be similar; to the extent that they had to address that gospel to a variety of issues facing the particular churches to whom they wrote, we may expect them to be different from each other.[11]

We may illustrate this idea with reference to the Third Gospel. Luke has long been noted for his interest in the oppressed. In Luke, more than in the other Gospels, Jesus appears as the friend of sinners and the savior of women.[12] The important issue is this: Did Luke create sayings and stories about women, the poor, the disadvantaged in order to make his point? Or did he draw these stories and sayings from his sources of material about Jesus? That is, was Luke being faithful to Jesus as he really was, or was Luke creating a largely fictitious person? I am convinced that Luke has underscored in special ways certain aspects of Jesus' historical public ministry by choosing to narrate a relatively large number of events having to do with Jesus and marginalized people.[13]

New Testament scholarship at its best, then, has demonstrated how the Gospels themselves want to be read—as purposeful documents. Their message arises out of the materials selected and the writers' interpretation of history. They do not intend precision in chronological details or in reproducing "what actually happened" or "what was really said."

A Lesson from the Visual Arts

A helpful way of making sense of this idea is to draw on analogies from the visual arts.[14] How might Jesus be portrayed? A photograph might be taken, and in this case we would have a relatively objective view of the historical person. Or an abstract painting might be made. This medium would provide us with only the vaguest impression of Jesus—if in fact we could recognize him at all. Alternatively, an artist might paint a portrait of Jesus—a medium which would be more selective than a photograph and which would allow for greater interpretive attention to certain details needing accentuation or de-emphasis.

The evangelists are best classified as "portrait artists." They were selective in their use of material about Jesus, and by combining their material in their own ways, they highlight certain features of Jesus' life and ministry. Hence, while each Gospel writer presents his own distinctive portrait of Jesus, clearly the same historical figure is portrayed by all.

Conclusion

The Gospels, then, are Good News. They tell the story of God's redemptive work in the life, ministry, death and resurrection of Jesus. In their pages we encounter the work and words of Jesus through whom we have salvation and in whom we base our faith. This good news is expressed in story form; yet, it has the power to lay its divine claim on our lives and call for the same life-changing response and commitment first proclaimed long ago by Jesus.

We are not laying aside for long the important issues raised in this chapter. Indeed, we have done little more than ask the appropriate questions and set the agenda for a closer look at the nature of the Gospels. The fundamental point on which we have focused here is that *the Gospels are purposeful documents.* In doing so we have demonstrated that two relatively common approaches to their interpretation are in fact misapproaches. Neither perspective takes into account the uniqueness of the Gospels as Gospels. These writings intend to communicate a particular message about Jesus and elicit particular responses from their readers. They are, in other words, good news.

5
The Gospels
as
History

———

Wide gulfs divide modern students of the Bible over how
we should regard the historical events described in the Gospels.
Thus, for example, while some church groups might regard the
details of the Gospel narratives of Jesus' last night before his
crucifixion—how he behaved, when he spoke and remained
silent, and what he said—as factual accounts, numerous other
persons, like George Wesley Buchanan, assert that neither we
nor the first evangelists have any historical knowledge of those
events.[1]

In the last century the question of the nature of the Gospels
has loomed large in scholarly circles, and no related issue has
stirred up more emotion and debate than the widespread denial that in the Gospels we encounter "what really happened."
More than eighty years ago, the German scholar William Wrede
pointed out for the first time the *theological character* of the Synoptic Gospels. Specifically, Wrede argued that in writing his
Gospel Mark was ruled by his theological program, and not by
historical considerations.[2] Even though Wrede's thesis did not
escape subsequent criticism and amendment, his general approach to understanding the nature of the Gospels is now wide-

ly accepted. After all, it is said,

> the early Christian gospels are not historical biographies of
> Jesus, and they do not provide the information necessary for
> constructing a "life" of Jesus. They are "gospels," that is, they
> *proclaim* a religious *message* about Jesus in narrative form.
> They express the significance which the early Christians
> found in Jesus. . . . In short, the gospels are primarily valu-
> able for what they tell us about what the early Christians
> *believed* about Jesus.[3]

This is not to say, however, that the church at large (or even
every New Testament scholar!) has adopted this position.

Faced with this skepticism regarding the historical trustworthiness of the Gospel accounts, modern Christians are sometimes
tempted to simply appeal to a preconceived idea about the
nature or origin of the Bible. According to their argument,
inasmuch as the Bible is God's Word, the Gospels must not be
questioned regarding their historical character. Or, since the
Bible is inerrant, the Gospels must be factual records.

Arguments of this sort, however, are unlikely to convince
anyone who does not already share similar presuppositions.
Moreover, this kind of argument is largely circular, for it pre-
scribes beforehand the reliability of the Gospel material. We
must recognize that our understanding of the *nature* of Scripture must take into account the data provided by the Scriptures
themselves.[4] For this reason, we must ask *whether the Gospels
themselves intend history.* Were the evangelists interested in reporting historical events? What evidence is available to us for
arguing that the Gospels are historical?

The Gospels: Preaching with History

In fact, much evidence supports the historical character of the
Gospels.[5] In the first place, we may take note of the bare fact
that what we have to do with here are, after all, *Gospels*—that
is, narratives concerned with Jesus' ministry. If the early church
had not been interested in the historical events of the life of
Jesus, then it is doubtful that the Gospel form of literature
would ever have been conceived. In all probability there existed

early on in the life of the church collections of Jesus' sayings— sayings which were unrelated to any specific historical context.[6] By their form and content such collections would have emphasized Jesus' role as revealer of divine truth, but they would have had little to say about the life of Jesus per se. Why did the evangelists move beyond this form of presenting the message of Jesus, unless they were interested in presenting something about Jesus' life?

Second, because Jesus' words were vested with special authority following his resurrection and even during his ministry, they along with stories about Jesus were carefully remembered and promulgated among the early Christians.[7] Jesus was not a typical rabbi: the Gospel of Mark itself records that the crowds were amazed at his teaching "because he taught them as one having authority, not as the teachers of the law" (1:22). The novelty of his ministry amid the teachers of his day is also seen in the depth of commitment required of his followers: he required absolute allegiance. Thus he would have regarded his teaching as vitally important. Consequently, he deliberately taught (using the normal educational techniques of his day) in forms that his audiences could easily remember.

His close disciples no doubt would have been trained as bearers of his teaching. In fact, we have every reason to expect that, as persons actively involved in his work, the disciples were tutored for this ministry. The Gospels themselves tell us that the disciples were involved in missionary activity during Jesus' own lifetime and that Jesus gave them both authority and instructions for their mission (see, for example, Mk 6:7-13, 30). Their proclamation was molded after Jesus' preaching about the kingdom of God and repentance.

More evidence along these lines is found in three other New Testament texts—Acts 10:34-43, Mark 1:1 and 1 John 1:1-2. First, the passage in Acts suggests that details concerning Jesus' earthly ministry had an important place in the early Christian mission. It has long been noted that the outline of Jesus' ministry in the Acts text shares the same basic framework of the Gospel of Mark.[8] Both begin the story of Jesus' ministry with reference to John the Baptist. In both, Jesus' baptism by John is explicitly regarded as an anointing by the Spirit. Following this reference to an event in Jesus' life, the sermon in Acts alludes in a general way to the earthly ministry of Jesus. Here, then, we have a summary of the "life of Jesus," with special emphasis on his death and resurrection (that is, a mini-Gospel), in the context of a missionary sermon.[9] This argues strongly for the idea that historical data about the life of Jesus was important in the early Christian mission.[10]

The second text, Mark 1:1, is equally important for assessing early Christian interest in the events of Jesus' life. A look at any good commentary will indicate the large degree of debate associated with the precise meaning of this "heading" in relation to the whole of Mark's writing. Nevertheless, one point seems beyond denial. For Mark, "the gospel" is the proclamation of the events and importance of Jesus' mission—his life, death and resurrection. That is, when Mark writes *gospel* in his opening clause, he is referring to the summation of Jesus' life from his baptism, down the long and dark path to the Place of the Skull, to the empty tomb.

Of course, for us modern Christians this emphasis may seem rather passé. After all, we associate the term *gospel* quite naturally with the writing projects of Matthew, Mark, Luke and John. However, from what we know about the early church, Mark's literary achievement in producing his Gospel is quite extraordinary. He took a term employed by the apostle Paul, which for Paul had primarily to do with the death and resurrection of Jesus, and affixed it to his dramatization of the *whole ministry of Jesus.* Hence, even if, as we have indicated, the early Christian mission drew on the life of Jesus in its proclamation, Mark's literary accomplishment is nothing less than innovative. By titling his story of Jesus a "Gospel," Mark demonstrates for us the importance of the events of Jesus life (even if they are often interpreted events) in apostolic Christianity.

The third text to examine is 1 John 1:1-2. The writer of this epistle (or tract) was apparently faced with a party who denied the true humanity of Jesus (see especially 1 Jn 4:2; 2 Jn 7). Thus, already in his opening address, he was at pains to declare the certainty and centrality of the earthly life of Jesus:

It was there from the beginning—that which we have heard, which we have beheld with our own eyes, which we have looked upon, which we have touched with our own hands—this which we proclaim concerning the word of life. The life appeared: we have seen it; we testify to it and proclaim to you the eternal life which was with the Father and has appeared to us. (1 Jn 1:1-2)

Without detailing the life of Jesus, our author makes clear in no uncertain terms the profound significance of Jesus' earthly life. In fact, it is as though he wants to communicate to his readers that the *message* of life is not to be separated from *that life*, the life of Jesus (see Jn 11:25; 14:6). The gospel about which 1 John will bear witness, then, "is the good news of a God who has disclosed himself uniquely in the historical person of Jesus."[11]

What we are suggesting, then, is that the evangelists fully intended to preach the Christian message by means of relating historical events. Accordingly, only a false dichotomy insists on separating the historical and theological elements of these early Christian writings. As Martin Hengel has argued,

the fatal error in the interpretation of the Gospels in general and of Mark in particular has been that scholars have thought that they had to decide between preaching and historical narration, that here there could only be an either-or. In reality the "theological" contribution of the evangelist lies in the fact that he combines these things inseparably: he preaches by narrating; he writes history and in so doing proclaims.[12]

It is true that the historical events narrated in the Gospels and Acts are more often than not couched in some sort of interpretive framework. This is seen most clearly in the birth and passion narratives, where Old Testament language and models are especially concentrated to bring out the significance of the story.[13] Likewise, the evangelists are selective in the stories they relate. Thus, except for a few verses in the Third Gospel, we read practically nothing in all four Gospels of Jesus' early life. We are uncertain about such seemingly important details as the date of Jesus' birth, his age at the beginning of his ministry and so on.

The narrative in Acts is also often painfully lacking in detail. Did Luke know of Paul's achievements in letter writing? What about the development of the early Christian mission apart from Paul? Luke does not answer these questions nor does he deal with scores of other issues we might like to raise. He tells us what *he* thinks is important. He, like the other Gospel writers, selects his material to make the point *he* is concerned to make. The evangelists preach with history. In doing so they have numerous historical precedents—especially among the historical writers of the Old Testament and of intertestamental Judaism who had already welded together factual event and theological interpretation.

Luke-Acts: Theology and History

In order to illustrate the historical nature of the Gospels we will pay special attention to the two parts of Luke's writing project, the Gospel of Luke and the Acts of the Apostles. Since the historical character of the Gospel of John is widely contested, we will turn more particularly to it at the close of this chapter.

Any discussion of the purpose of Luke-Acts must take as its point of departure Luke's own statement of intention—Luke 1:1-4:[14]

> Inasmuch as many have undertaken to compile an account of the events which have been fulfilled among us, just as they have been passed on to us by those who were from the beginning eyewitnesses and servants of the word, I too have decided, after having carefully investigated everything from the beginning, to write an orderly account for you, most excellent Theophilus, in order that you may know the certainty of the things about which you have been informed.

This is a rather complex and bulky sentence and we will not attempt to mine its riches exhaustively. Rather, we will focus on only the issues it raises which have direct bearing on Luke's interest in history. In the first place, we cannot help noting that this statement of intent has its parallel in the opening of the Acts of the Apostles:

> In my first book, O Theophilus, I wrote about all that Jesus began to do and teach until the day when, having instructed through the Holy Spirit the apostles whom he had chosen, he was taken up into heaven. (1:1-2)

On the basis of the preface in Luke and its counterpart in Acts we are certainly correct in regarding Luke and Acts as a unified work in two volumes.[15] What is more, we gain here a clear indication that Luke was interested in telling what he regarded as the *whole* story of the rise of the Gospel—both its beginnings in the earthly mission of Jesus, from his birth to his ascension, and its continuation in the early Christian mission. In this he goes beyond the purposes of the other evangelists, for he wants to demonstrate the continuity between what happened prior to *and following* Jesus' ascension.

Luke's statement of purpose also suggests to us the care with which he conducted his research. His investigation, he says, has been thorough (that is, from the beginning), complete and accurate. Moreover, he has gained information from eyewitnesses and ministers of the word (apostles?), and has drawn on his own observations about the spread of the church. In this regard remember that among ancient writers of history, when personal observation was impossible, reliable writing depended above all on eyewitness testimony.[16] Here we have Luke's self-assessment of his literary work: he has done his homework, and he has done it well.

But Luke is also quick to point out that he is not solely interested in providing a factual account as though he were a mere chronicler or bookkeeper. He does this by making use of the technical language of fulfillment. That is, into a lengthy introductory sentence noted for its points of contact with Hellenistic historical writing and classical Greek, Luke implants an expression, "the things which have been fulfilled," that smacks of the promise-fulfillment language of Israelite religion. The events about which he writes, we are told, must be seen against the backdrop of Old Testament anticipation. Luke plans to recount the fulfillment of God's promises in Jesus and the early church.

Finally, we must note the person to whom Luke addresses his work. Whether Theophilus was already a schooled Christian or had only heard bits and pieces of the gospel continues to be debated. Regardless of how one answers this question, however, it remains that Luke is interested in confirming for Theophilus the accuracy of the church's gospel.

At the outset of Luke-Acts, then, Luke sets before his readers his own agenda—which is very much historical and theological. Of course, Luke's models for writing history were those of the ancient world, and their interests and standards were not necessarily those of our own day. Their approach can be illustrated by noting the standard Thucydides set for recording speeches:

> As to the speeches that were made by different men, either when they were about to begin the war or when they were already engaged therein, it has been difficult to recall with strict accuracy the words actually spoken, both for me as regards that which I myself heard, and for those who from various sources have brought me reports. Therefore the speeches are given in the language which, as it seemed to me, the several speakers would express, on the subjects under consideration, the sentiments most befitting the occasion, though at the same time I have adhered as closely as possible to the general sense of what was actually said. *(History of the Peloponnesian War, 1. 22. 1)*

According to this statement of method, Thucydides *both* aimed for accuracy, reporting the essence of the various speeches, *and* apparently saw nothing wrong with reporting speeches he had never heard. In fact, in his historical narrative the orators speak the language of Thucydides, the speeches are too short to be actual, and some appear abruptly in their context. Hence, Thucydides adopted a method which gave him latitude in the recording of speeches, a method with room for both objective and subjective elements. Although Thucydides lived some 450 years before Luke, comparisons of his work with that of subsequent historians indicate that the science of history writing did not change substantially in the intervening years. Naturally, then, we cannot insist on testing Luke's ability to fulfill his historical aims by measuring his two volumes against the relatively new standards of strict accuracy expected of contemporary historians.

Throughout this discussion I have referred to the author of the Third Gospel and the Acts of the Apostles as Luke. In fact, these two volumes are anonymous, as are the other Gospels. Nowhere in Luke-Acts does the author identify himself explicitly (as, for example, Paul does in Rom 1:1). The traditional titles attributing the authorship of the four Gospels to Matthew, Mark, Luke and John were added to each of the Gospels only later.

On the one hand, we could follow tradition and simply refer to the author of Luke-Acts as Luke without committing ourselves on the problem of whether this Luke is to be identified with Paul's companion (see Col 4:14; Philem 24; 2 Tim 4:11). On the other, with respect to the general historical character of certain aspects of the narrative in Acts, this is not an unimportant question. That is, if we can say with some confidence that the author of Luke-Acts was Paul's companion, then it will be even more clear that he had personal knowledge of many of the events mentioned in his narrative.

Apart from the rather extensive church tradition identifying Luke as Paul's companion (the earliest of which dates into the second century), the material evidence at hand is found in the Acts of the Apostles.[17] At several points in the latter half of that narrative (16:10-17; 20:5-15; 21:1-18; 27:1—28:16) the author begins to write in the first person, relating what "we" did. Could it be that the writer is here working from his own diary of his travels with the apostle Paul, or at least identifying himself as one of Paul's companions?

Given the otherwise observable care with which the author of Luke-Acts smooths out differences in style among his sources, these passages most likely are to be understood autobiographically.[18] In all probability, Paul did travel with groups (see, for example, Philem 23-24; Gal 1:2), and it is generally agreed that among known companions of Paul, Luke is the most likely candidate for the narrator of Acts. This, taken together with the consistent designation of Luke as the author of the Third Gospel in the early tradition, speaks in favor of our identification of the author of the Third Gospel and Acts as Luke, one of Paul's companions.

It is beyond the scope of this chapter to begin a treatment of the historical character of the Gospel of Luke and the Acts of the Apostles in any detail. We may note, however, that the historical value of the Acts has especially come under fire in the last two centuries. Yet, even here a growing body of evidence is being gathered in support of its trustworthiness both in matters of detail and in getting the larger picture correct. Readers interested in pursuing problems of this nature in greater depth are encouraged to study carefully the commentaries on Luke and Acts by Howard Marshall—which pay special attention to such questions, and Ward Gasque's survey of the study of Acts.[19]

Epilogue: History in John
The long-observed distinctiveness of John's Gospel when compared with the others has raised serious questions about its relative value as a historical document. From early Christian times it was regarded as the "spiritual Gospel," and numerous readers have seen in it a much more developed and in some cases more profound interpretation of Jesus' ministry than that found in the Synoptic Gospels. Not only in the theology or chronology of the Gospel (see, for example, the relative positioning of the account of the cleansing of the temple), but even in the form in which Jesus' sayings are transmitted, the fourth evangelist goes his own way.

Thus, in John, Jesus does not speak primarily in parables, brief sayings and controversy dialogs as in the first three Gospels, but in lengthy discourses. Here, Jesus is much more open about his identity, mission and relation to the Father than in the other Gospels, and he uses unparalleled expressions (see, for example, the "I am" sayings). For such reasons as these,

New Testament scholars have long doubted or outright denied the usefulness of the Gospel of John for understanding the historical character of Jesus' ministry.[20] It is worth noting, however, that New Testament scholars did not conjure up this problem, but only observed that the Gospel of John looks different from the Synoptic Gospels. That is, the Fourth Gospel itself poses the problem by its form and content.

The publication of C. H. Dodd's study *Historical Tradition in the Fourth Gospel* marked something of a watershed in the study of the historical value of the Gospel of John.[21] He, along with other interpreters before and since, argued that the Gospel of John was everywhere dependent on valuable, historical, non-Synoptic material. The use of independent tradition, he argued, explains the divergence in the respective portrayals of Jesus' ministry.

Moreover, John's accuracy with regard to historical, social and geographical details has now been widely recognized, and this has raised an important question: Would we not expect an author who gets it right on minor points (which can be verified by external evidence) to exercise similar care at major points (which often cannot)? At the very least we must recognize from his accuracy on geographical matters that John's material is firmly rooted in reliable tradition of some kind.

Another factor worth considering arises out of John 1:14: the author of the Fourth Gospel straightforwardly identifies himself as an eyewitness, one who has "seen his glory, the glory of the one and only Son." Regardless of whether one is able to identify the author of this Gospel with the apostle John himself, it thus seems clear that his authority and witness stand behind it.

Of course, on the other hand, it cannot be denied that the fourth evangelist is willing to unfold the message and significance of Jesus in ways which single his work out. For example, while hints of Christ's pre-existent status might be uncovered in the Synoptics, no doubt on this point is left in John's Gospel (see 1:1, 14). Nevertheless, as Earle Ellis has helpfully reminded us, "his interpretation arises out of events which he believes actually to have occurred."[22]

Conclusion

For the purpose of understanding the character of the Gospels it is important to ask the sorts of historical questions we have been raising in this chapter. If the Gospels do intend history, as we have argued, then it is important to attempt to read them as such and within their own historical ethos. Also, for the purpose of having adequate grounding for our faith it is important to ask questions regarding the historical character of the Gospels. After all, our faith has as its object a God whom, we believe, invaded history in a profoundly particular manner—in the person of Jesus of Nazareth. We must remember, nevertheless, that historical inquiry can never "prove" faith. Thus, for example, while historical investigation might be able to demonstrate that Jesus was in fact crucified under Pontius Pilate, only faith can take the further step of grasping the theological significance of that death as a vicarious atonement for sin (that is, "that Christ died for our sins"—1 Cor 15:3). At some point we must move on to discover more than the Jesus behind the Gospels; we must come face to face with the Jesus of the Gospels—the Jesus whose significance can only be understood in light of his resurrection and continual lordship.

6
The Gospels
as
Theology

Who was Jesus? In order to answer this question, we might be tempted to write an essay, pen a song, draw a picture or relate our own experience of the Risen Lord. Matthew, Mark, Luke and John—they wrote Gospels. Drawing on materials of all kinds—written and oral, isolated stories and extended collections, brief sayings and narrative accounts—they wrote stories, addressing the question, Who was Jesus?

Obviously, these evangelists were not interested only in mere facts and events. Who was Jesus? For them, an adequate answer to this question must move beyond a résumé of Jesus' activities. A further issue must be addressed. So what? In their minds, a description of who Jesus was necessarily included discussion of his significance—for his time and theirs. However, rather than add an addendum to their stories—a prosaic treatise detailing in systematic fashion the significant theological points of the meaning of Jesus' life, death and resurrection—they simply told the story. In constructing their narratives, they related *event* and *significance* inseparably, at one and the same time. For this, the evangelists have been recognized as artists and interpreters. In the past twenty-five years, they have increasingly been regarded as theologians.

Jesus' Mockery: Event and Interpretation

One helpful illustration of the way in which event and interpretation are welded together in the Gospels is the story of how the soldiers mocked Jesus in Mark 15:17-19. After Pilate sentenced Jesus to be crucified, Jesus was flogged and led away into the palace. After this, the soldiers "put a purple robe on him, then wove a crown of thorns and set it on him. And they began to call out to him, 'Hail, King of the Jews!' Again and again they struck him on the head with a staff and spit on him. Falling on their knees, they worshiped him."

Two points are of particular interest here. First, it is notable that in mocking Jesus as a pretender to the throne the soldiers refer to him as "King of the Jews." In hailing him as king and paying him homage, they ironically identify Jesus correctly! Unwittingly, they make themselves confessors of Jesus' true identity. This irony would not have been lost on early Christians who read this account.

Second, we observe that a typological identification has been made between Jesus and the Servant of the Lord from Isaiah. In the Greek version of Isaiah 50:6, we read: "I offered my back to the whips, my cheeks to blows; I did not turn my face from mocking and spitting." The relation between the two figures—Jesus and the Servant—is obvious: Both are struck, mocked and spat on.

On the basis of these theological observations, some scholars might be tempted to discount the historicity of this event. Could it be that Mark simply made up this story in order to identify Jesus as the King and as the Servant? This appears highly unlikely for several reasons, the most important being this: a scene of mockery such as this has parallels in ancient history.[1] Thus Philo, a contemporary of the apostle Paul, records how an imbecile named Carabas was paid homage and addressed as "Lord."[2] Likewise, there is a story from the first century A.D. in which the Persians placed a condemned man on the throne at a festival occasion, allowing him to exercise a mock rule.

Therefore, we see how Mark has reported an event, but not simply as a chronicler or bookkeeper might. In recounting the

story of Jesus' mockery before the Roman soldiers, he has combined event and interpretation. By making use of the rhetorical
device of irony, and by wording his account in a way designed
to bring to mind the text from Isaiah, he has employed history
to make a theological point. In unexpected ways, the event of
the mockery serves to identify Jesus as King of the Jews and as
the Servant of the Lord. It is not enough to tell us what happened; Mark also tells us the significance of what happened.

A Christian Perspective

To regard the writers of the Gospels as theologians may be
difficult for some persons. After all, with the Gospels we are not
dealing with pieces of literature comparable to Calvin's *Institutes*
or Barth's *Church Dogmatics.* We might be tempted to think that
the evangelists accomplished something totally unique in their
marriage of event and interpretation. In fact, while the evangelists were innovators in many ways, drawing together into an
inseparable bond history and its significance, they were hardly
blazing a new trail. There are numerous other parallels, ancient and modern.

Earlier, we noted that the historians of ancient Israel were
interested in relating events in the life of the nation *in terms of
God's activity.* In this way, they paved the way for the important
task of the Gospel writers. While not necessarily pointing to the
significance of divine activity, the earliest Greek historians did
write their histories for instructive purposes. Greek historians
such as Thucydides and Polybius wrote their works with an eye
toward being faithful to the actual events—while at the same
time imparting political, military and economic wisdom.

Historians today are no less interested in the significance of
the events and times they study. For example, in their study of
Scotland's history, P. and F. S. Fry write:

In the last years of the seventeenth century the Scots found
themselves drifting towards full political union with England,
but it was a union few people in Scotland wanted. They
feared, rightly as it turned out, that it would be a 'take-over,'
to use a twentieth-century term. And when it did come, most

of the advantages were stacked on England's side.[3]
The perspective of these authors is clear, but their attitude may
come as something of a surprise to North American readers
unaware of the sometimes intense nationalistic feelings shared
by many Scots. No doubt, similar biases could be observed from
a reading of the stories of the Civil War as respectively told by
historians of the Union and of the Confederacy. Alternatively,
we might simply compare maps of the earth produced in the
United States with those produced in Australia or New Zealand,
noting especially which land mass appears as the "center of the
world!" Ancient and modern people, historians and lay folk—
all perceive the times through their own perspectives, and this
influences the way these events and people are recounted.

The Gospel writers have their own general perspective. They
write as Christians, persons who believe that the historical man
Jesus lives on as the Risen Lord. They write from the stance of
their own faith, attempting to shed light on the events of Jesus'
life (and, in the case of Luke, also on the growth of the church).
More than this, they write in particular historical situations,
with particular people in mind. They write to counter some
ideas or to encourage others, to draw out the meaning of the
gospel story for their own audiences. For this reason, we may
justifiably regard them as theologians.

An Imperative for Interpretation
Because the evangelists are also theologians, Christians today
who are interested in correctly interpreting the Gospels are
given at least one, clear methodological direction. When reading Matthew's Gospel, we must try to understand Matthew's
Gospel *on its own*. We must attempt to understand what *Matthew*
was trying to say by the way he told the story. Mark, Luke and
John must be allowed their own integrity as well.

This is not to say that we should not compare the Gospel
accounts. Indeed, I argued in chapter two that the reality of
having *four* Gospels and not *one* demanded that we compare the
Gospel narratives. But the purpose of such comparison is not
to harmonize the accounts, but rather to draw attention to the

peculiarities of each. What I am saying here, then, is that when studying the message of any one Gospel, we must turn our back on any temptation to fill in the story of that Gospel with details taken from the others. Each Gospel has its own distinctive message, inspired by the Holy Spirit, and our task as readers of each of the Gospels is to grasp that message and allow it to lay its claim on our lives.

This ability of the evangelists to emphasize their own concerns while telling the same story is well illustrated by Mark's and Matthew's versions of the story of the woman with a hemorrhage. In both renditions this episode is sandwiched in the midst of the narrative of the healing of the daughter of a ruler (Jairus, according to Mark). We will pick up the story with Jesus en route to the home of the ruler.

Mark 5:24-34 (NIV)

A large crowd followed and pressed around him. And a woman was there who had been subject to bleeding for twelve years. She had suffered a great deal under the care of many doctors and had spent all that she had, yet instead of getting better she grew worse. When she heard about Jesus, she came up behind him in the crowd and touched his cloak, because she thought, "If I just touch his clothes, I will be healed." Immediately her bleeding stopped; and she felt in her body that she was freed from her suffering. At once Jesus realized that power had gone out from him. He turned around in the crowd and said, "Who touched my clothes?" "You see the people crowding against you," his disciples answered, "and yet you can ask, 'Who touched me?' " But Jesus kept looking around to see who had done it. Then the woman, knowing what had happened to her, came and fell at his feet

Matthew 9:19-22 (NIV)

Jesus got up and went with him, and so did his disciples. Just then a woman who had been subject to bleeding for twelve years

came up behind him and touched the edge of his cloak. She said to herself, "If I only touch his cloak, I will be healed."

and, trembling with fear, told
him the whole truth. He said
to her, "Daughter, your faith
has healed you. Go in peace
and be freed from your
suffering."

Jesus turned and saw her.
"Take heart, daughter," he said,
"your faith has healed you."
And the woman was healed from
that moment.

What immediately strikes us about these two renditions is the rather pointed differences in length. Mark's version is much longer and, consequently, contains much more descriptive detail than Matthew's. On the other hand, it is equally obvious that both evangelists are relating the same story.

When comparing different renditions of the same story, we begin to see the different emphases of the evangelists. In this case, Matthew has presented his version in greatly abbreviated form, with the dominant emphasis falling on Jesus. No details detract from Jesus, and he is presented as the majestic one who is able to save a believer. (In the Gospels Jesus' delivering a person from physical distress is often a sign of his or her salvation.) The final phrase ("And the woman was healed from that moment") has been added by Matthew to make clear that the moment of the woman's healing was when Jesus spoke to her. It also stresses the immediacy and permanence of her salvation.

Mark's interests are not contradictory to Matthew's, but his presentation underscores this idea in different ways. His version embraces other points of interest as well. In Mark, for example, we are struck by the magnitude of the woman's problem: all human efforts had been exhausted, all possibilities tried, and she was only getting worse. Human efforts had failed. Something else was needed. That "something else" was Jesus' power, divine power. And lest it appear that Jesus served only as some sort of conduit for this power, Mark's story points out that he was conscious that a healing had taken place. In fact, Jesus was very much in control of the whole event, as demonstrated by the fact that his words were required to confirm the healing and approve the woman's action, motivated as it was by faith.

In addition, Mark records the response of the disciples to

Jesus' question, "Who touched my garment?" In doing so Mark gives the reader an indication that the disciples lacked perception into Jesus' person and mission—an important motif in Mark. This emphasis is completely lacking in Matthew's version.

Hence, we see that the *way* the evangelists tell their stories is guided by their own interests, their own theology. Even though the theologies of both stories intersect at the point of the woman's faith, the presence or absence of other details provides additional theological insight.

We have thus seen how different perspectives might be incorporated by the various evangelists when relating the same episode. In this chapter, we will illustrate the theological character of the Gospels on a grander scale with special reference to the Fourth Gospel. In order to assist readers of the other Gospels, we will also mention their central themes, though without developing them in any detail.

The Gospel of John as Theology

Why did John write his Gospel?[4] What message did he intend to communicate? What makes John's *Gospel John's* Gospel? Rather than attempt an artificial categorization of John's thought, we will examine John's understanding of the gospel in the context of his writing. While we will bring into view other pertinent texts and themes, our own inquiry will center especially on two texts: John 20:30-31 and John 9:1-41.

John 20:30-31. At the close of his chapter 20, the evangelist provides his readers with his own statement of purpose. As we shall see momentarily, this statement, while apparently limited in scope, is in fact important for our understanding of John's purpose and the structure of his Gospel. He writes: "Jesus did many other miraculous signs in the presence of his disciples, which are not recorded in this book. But these are written that you may believe that Jesus is the Christ, the Son of God, and that by believing you may have life in his name" (NIV).

In this statement John makes clear that he has included in his Gospel only a portion of the available material and that he

was guided in his selection by a definite purpose.[5] But what
purpose? We may outline a few observations as follows.

1. There is some ambiguity regarding the phrase "that you
may believe" in verse 31. Should we understand John to be
writing to unbelievers "in order that you might believe for the
first time"? Or, is he writing to Christians "so that you might
continue to believe"?[6] Common sense might suggest to us that
no rigid distinction need be made between these two options
in terms of John's purpose. After all, a modern evangelist like
Luis Palau might deliver a message designed to bring people
into the faith, but which also encourages and instructs those
who are already Christians. This line of thinking is actually
supported by the content of the Fourth Gospel. Some stories,
such as Jesus' miraculous signs, seem to be told in order to
evoke faith. Other parts of the Gospel, however, such as the
extended farewell discourse (Jn 14—17), seem better suited for
believers. We may justifiably generalize: John intends to present Jesus in such a way that faith will be encouraged.

2. We may ask, Faith in what? There is no ambiguity regarding the answer to this question. John's primary objective is
Christological; he intends to encourage faith in Jesus *as* the
Christ, the Son of God. John, then, is not interested in merely
recounting Jesus' life. Rather, he intends to demonstrate by his
selection and arrangement of material that Jesus is the Christ,
the Son of God. His Gospel, he hopes, will encourage faith in
this Jesus.

Confessing Christ had important repercussions for John's
readers. For them, an acknowledgment of this kind meant ex-
clusion from the Jewish synagogue, and so it was not made
lightly (see Jn 9:22; 12:42; 16:2). Apparently, some among
John's audience were Jewish Christians (and, perhaps, Jews
who remained "closet Christians") faced with opposition from
Jews in their own communities. The Fourth Evangelist hopes
to equip such readers for their encounter with Jewish objec-
tions and opposition, and to strengthen them in their claim of
Jesus' messiahship.[7]

In this text the title "Son of God" is closely associated with the title "Christ." John has probably included both here because one would be more meaningful to some of his readers, the other to others. Nevertheless, "Son of God" is the most pervasive way of designating Jesus in the Gospel of John, and it focuses sharply the all-important Father-Son relationship developed in John. In this respect, a quick look at the introduction to the Gospel will prove helpful.

In terms of its function in the whole Gospel, the prologue—John 1:1-18—might seem something of a mystery. After all, its central emphasis on the "Word" ("Logos") is found nowhere else in the Gospel narrative itself, and we might rightly wonder why John opened his account with this more speculative statement. The key to this dilemma is in verses 14 and 18, for there it becomes clear that the Word is actually the Son, Jesus. In other words, John uses late Jewish speculation about the Word in order to introduce Jesus the Son in pre-eminently exalted terms. This otherworldly side of Jesus is apparent throughout John's Gospel; even in the story of Jesus' suffering and death he appears very much in control (see, for example, Jn 18:2-11).

As the Son, Jesus is portrayed in John's Gospel as having dwelt in heaven, having been sent by the Father into the world in order to bring salvation, having ministered in the world while carrying out the divine functions but in obedience to the Father, and having been exalted in his death. We might diagram John's understanding of Jesus' career as the Son in this way:

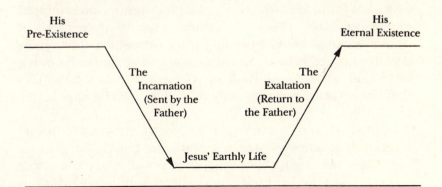

His
Pre-Existence

His
Eternal Existence

The
Incarnation
(Sent by the
Father)

The
Exaltation
(Return to
the Father)

Jesus' Earthly Life

John's purpose then is to present as the object of faith this Jesus who is the only true Son of God.

How important this purpose-statement is for understanding the shape and theology of John's Gospel is suggested by the parallel verse in 12:37: "Even after Jesus had done all these miraculous signs in their presence, they still would not believe in him" (NIV).

Prior to this statement, Jesus had performed all of the miraculous signs John records. Yet, as John here summarizes, Jesus' miracles had come in for mixed reviews. Some believed but many doubted. By returning to the theme of miraculous signs and belief in 20:30-31 John is saying, in effect: Those earlier miracles were not enough. Changing the water into wine, multiplying the loaves, even restoring a dead man to life—these are insufficient to elicit faith. Something more is required. Some other "sign" is necessary. What is that sign? What alone is adequate to give rise to faith? The last sign is this: The Son of Man being lifted up on the cross to die (see above all, 3:13-15; also 8:28; 12:23, 34-36; 13:31; et al.). That is, for John, Jesus' death is the most profound revelation of Jesus' identity, and this revelation leads to faith.

3. What is the result of faith? John asserts that the end of faith is "life in his name." Life, often designated in the Fourth Gospel as "eternal life," is the consistent expression with which John refers to salvation. Life is not merely to be anticipated in some future eternity, but begins at the moment of belief. In the Gospel of John, life is the result of faith in Jesus, who is himself the bearer of life. This is the central meaning of the series of "I am" sayings found only in John's Gospel; in them Jesus declares himself to be in an ultimate way what men and women need and seek. As in Paul, so in John, the salvation (life) brought by Jesus is inseparably related to the Holy Spirit (see Jn 14, 16).

In the end, John is concerned with salvation—and in this he is certainly at one with Matthew, Mark and Luke.[8]

4. Someone might object that this expression of intent, "that you may have life," is itself quite general and hardly brings us

in touch with the distinctiveness of John's thought. We may expand our horizon somewhat by noticing that this statement of purpose follows directly on the heels of Thomas's confession of faith in the Risen Lord.

This story, from which we gain the expression "Doubting Thomas," narrates Thomas's reluctance to believe that Jesus had been raised from the dead until after his own encounter with the Resurrected One. At this, he acknowledges Jesus as Lord and God (Jn 20:28). Jesus then responds, "Is it because you have seen me that you have believed? Blessed are those who do not see and yet believe!" In effect, Jesus puts aside the effectiveness of "physical sight" for inspiring faith. Indeed, as we have observed, throughout the Gospel of John, Jesus' miracles are only partially successful in encouraging faith. Some kind of perception other than physical is necessary then.

In other words, with or without sight of the figure of Jesus on earth, faith is supremely a matter of spiritual perception. And, the fourth evangelist comments, this Gospel is written with precisely such an aim in mind—that, on the basis of the evidence marshaled, his readers may have eyes to see that Jesus is the life-giving Messiah and Son of God.[9]

In this way, every successive generation of readers—readers without the opportunity to have an encounter with the earthly Jesus—are addressed and called to exercise spiritual perception. And this brings us to our second text.

John 9:1-41. If in the previous section we looked at an explicit statement of John's theological purpose, here we have an opportunity to see him in action as an interpreter of the gospel. Of the many tools used by John and the other evangelists to communicate their message in narrative form, which we will look at in more detail in the next two chapters, two are worthy of special mention now. First, we cannot help but be impressed by the sheer length of this story—especially given its humble beginnings in verses 1-7. If this were a simple miracle account, such as the many related in the Synoptic Gospels, we would expect the narrative to move on to another episode in verse 8. That it does not do so and that we must wait some thirty-three verses (until Jn 10:1) for a shift in content suggests to us the importance of the point John drives home here.

Incidentally, the closely interrelated character of the segments in John 9:1-41 should also caution us against trying to understand John's theological message by studying bits and pieces of stories. A miracle story like this one must be seen in its larger context and, in the end, should be related to the overall message of the Gospel as a whole.

Second, a reading of John 9 reveals the progressive nature of the narrative in which the miracle story, verses 1-7, is only the starting point for a lengthy, message-laden account. We may outline the movement of the story as follows:

Verses 1-7:	Jesus heals a blind man.
Verses 8-12:	The man is questioned by his neighbors.
Verses 13-17:	The man is questioned by the Pharisees.
Verses 18-23:	The man's parents are questioned by the Pharisees.
Verses 24-34:	The man is questioned a second time by the Pharisees.
Verses 35-41:	Jesus dialogs with the Pharisees on the subject of blindness.

Unfortunately, while this outline demonstrates something of the repetition and flow of the chapter, it does not get at the heart of its progressive nature. It is not simply that different groups are involved in the detective work. John wants us to notice the shift in attitudes as the narrative progresses.

Follow the man healed of blindness. In the opening scene he says nothing and demonstrates no faith other than that required of him to wash his eyes in the pool of Siloam. In his first interrogation, he tells his neighbors only that a man called Jesus put mud on his eyes; he apparently knows nothing else about Jesus. In the third scene, he is prepared to designate Jesus as a prophet, no more. In the fourth, his parents come close to acknowledging Jesus as the Messiah, but are afraid to do so, and so defer to their son. In the fifth, he is portrayed as a man in opposition to the Pharisees—which, in the Fourth Gospel, marks him as a disciple already. Finally, in the last scene, he openly confesses his belief in Jesus and worships him.

Here we have a progressive unveiling of the man's faith toward Jesus. He gains physical sight *and* spiritual perception. Likewise, there is progression (or rather, regression) in the response of the man's questioners throughout the narrative—from a mild form of curiosity to a more and more hardened stance in opposition to Jesus.

Had we read verses 1-7 on their own, we might gain the impression that the point of the story would lead to a discussion of the presence of evil in the world. Already here, however, is a hint that the real point will be developed down another track, for in verse 5 we hear Jesus' declaration, "I am the light of the world." As it turns out, the whole chapter turns on distinctions between those who perceive and those who do not perceive this light.

In this respect we see a startling reversal of roles. The man who was blind now sees. The Pharisees demonstrated that though they have eyes to see, they are in fact blind. As the narrative unfolds, the blind man gains spiritual sight, and so is enabled to make his confession of faith. As the narrative unfolds, the Pharisees—who ought to have developed spiritual perception, and in fact claim to be reliable spiritual guides—refuse to believe and so prove to be blind. In this way we are prepared for the punch line:

Jesus said, "For judgment I have come into this world, so that the blind will see and those who see will become blind." Some Pharisees who were with him heard him say this and asked, "What? Are we blind too?" Jesus said, "If you were blind, you would not be guilty of sin; but now that you claim you can see, your guilt remains." (NIV)

By drawing us into the world of this narrative, John instructs us as to the meaning of Jesus' assertion, "I am the light of the world," and so we realize that in him alone is their true sight.

Epilogue: Matthew, Mark and Luke as Theologians
In the case of John's Gospel we were able to devote our atten-

tion at some length to the evangelist's explicit statement of purpose and suggest in the context of one passage how John the evangelist is an interpreter of the story of Jesus. We must deal much more summarily with the other Gospels, pointing only to their most significant theological interests.

Matthew. Perhaps the most prominent theme of the First Gospel is that Jesus is the promised Messiah—a motif which raises its head in the very first verse of the Gospel and influences the whole subsequent narrative.[10] In fact, the whole Gospel is built around the messiahship of Jesus. The structure of the First Gospel is marked off by Matthew's use of the phrase "from that time on Jesus began . . ." at two significant places in his narrative (4:17; 16:21). This formula divides the Gospel into three sections, each of which focuses on an aspect of Jesus' messiahship: The Person of Jesus the Messiah (1:1-4:16); The Proclamation of Jesus the Messiah (4:17-16:20); and The Suffering, Death and Resurrection of Jesus the Messiah (16:21-28:20).[11]

This emphasis on the messiahship of Jesus underscores the Jewish character of the Gospel, an emphasis also apparent in the Gospel's interesting use of the Old Testament. More than fifty explicit citations of the Hebrew Scriptures may be counted in Matthew. To this number we could add numerous allusions to Old Testament texts and people. In the opening chapters, for example, Matthew indicates how each major event in the narrative of Jesus' birth is a fulfillment of Scripture.[12]

The Jewish flavor of the Gospel according to Matthew should not cause us to overlook Matthew's obvious concern for Gentiles. The Great Commission embraces "all nations" (Mt 28:19-20), and it is a group of Gentiles ("magi from the East") who search out the Christ's birthplace (Mt 2:1-12). In fact, texts like 21:43 (where Jesus speaks of taking the good news to the Gentiles) suggest that this Gospel was not written for the Jews after all, but for a Christian community which grew out of Judaism. In the end, then, Matthew is really interested in the church of the Messiah (among the Gospel writers Matthew alone uses *ekklesia,* the Greek term for "church"). Indeed, one can hardly overlook the central role of Jesus as teacher in the First Gospel, and this is probably closely related to Matthew's interest in providing instruction for the organized church.

Mark. The second evangelist portrays the ministry of Jesus as a relentless progression of events leading to the crucifixion of the Messiah.[13] Mark makes no apology for this absurd turn of events (see 1 Cor 1:22-24), for it is precisely in his death that Jesus is revealed as the Son of God. Moreover, Mark demonstrates that Jesus' life, death and resurrection were all part of God's plan, as foretold in the Scriptures. In his death, Jesus instituted the community of the new covenant, obtaining salvation for those who follow him in sacrificial, other-oriented service.

One of the important questions appearing again and again in the Gospel of Mark is that concerning Jesus' identity. This question occurs in various forms, often in comparisons of Jesus with otherwise well-known things. It appears in various forms either explicitly (as in 1:22, 27; 4:41; 6:2-3) or implicitly (as in 2:7, 16, 24; 7:5). What kind of authority is this? Who is this that can do such things? From where does his authority come? This question is given its clearest expression by Jesus at Caesarea Philippi, where Jesus asks his disciples, "Who do you say I am?" (8:29).

At one level this is a Christological question—a question of Jesus' identity. That is, Mark is interested in his readers having a proper understanding of who Jesus is, and it is noteworthy that the major Christological titles for Jesus in Mark are interpreted in terms of Jesus' passion. The "Son of God" title is of utmost significance for Mark (see 1:1), but it is only in view of Jesus' crucifixion that any human in the Gospel acclaims Jesus with this title (15:39). The title "Messiah" (or "Christ") is also important. And in 8:29 Peter proclaims, "You are the Christ," but immediately thereafter Jesus interprets his messiahship in terms of suffering and death. The most pervasive title for Jesus in Mark, "Son of Man," is also regularly interpreted in terms of Jesus' passion—for example: "The Son of Man did not come to be served, but to serve, and to give his life as a ransom for many" (10:45 NIV; see also 8:31; 9:31; 10:33-34, where Jesus' resurrection as Son of Man is also anticipated).

On the other hand, it is equally clear that Mark is not interested in Christology alone; rather, he is interested in discipleship. What is the appropriate response to Jesus, the Christ, Son of God? How do we follow him in discipleship? In two texts, 8:27-38 and 10:35-45, this is made very clear, though elsewhere this theme is equally present. In these two passages the character of the obedient, other-oriented, suffering Messiah places its stamp on and defines the nature of the life of the disciple. Without a doubt, Mark has carefully linked Christology and discipleship. That is, in view of Jesus' steadfastness and obedience to the will of God in the face of suffering and death, Jesus' disciples are urged to exercise that same faithfulness while awaiting Jesus' return as the triumphant Son of Man.

Luke and Acts. In recent years, many Christians have underscored the social and political themes of the Gospel of Luke.[14] That such themes are present and important for Luke is certain, and we are indebted to such scholars for highlighting the challenge of his message for today's Christians in these areas. On the other hand, we must note that any discussion of the purpose of Luke's Gospel must take into consideration the fact that the Gospel is only the first of a two-part work. Hence, any statement of Luke's purpose must not sweep away from the discussion the Acts of the Apostles. When viewed as a whole, Luke-Acts emphasizes many themes worth developing and applying in our own day, but the overarching theme centers on salvation in Jesus Christ.

In this regard the programmatic character of the story of Jesus preaching in his hometown is more and more being recognized. In this scene Jesus reads from the Prophet Isaiah (61:1-2, with a line added from 58:6), and thus proclaims the favorable year of the Lord. This was the long-awaited ultimate Jubilee (borrowing from the theme of Lev 25), when God's final salvation would be realized. According to Jesus, this year, this anticipated time *has now come and is present in his proclamation and acts* (Lk 4:16-30). Later in Luke, Jesus uses these very images to demonstrate for the disciples of John that he was indeed the expected one (Lk 7:21-22).

In order to understand the full importance of this scene in Nazareth for the whole of Luke-Acts, we must recognize the source of the people's fury in rejecting Jesus' announcement. That he proclaimed "today is the expected day" was not the problem; this would have been a welcome announcement. The problem is that Jesus interpreted Isaiah's message in a universalistic way, offering Gentiles the emancipation of the kingdom. This is clear both from Jesus' use of Isaiah 58:6 in conjunction with Isaiah 61:1-2 in the Old Testament citation and from the references to the mission of Elijah and Elisha to non-Israelites in 4:26-27. That Israel risked judgment while Gentiles enjoyed the salvation of God—this was unwelcome news! Consequently, Jesus and his proclamation were rejected.

Yet precisely this message—the offering of the salvation of God to those whom "the chosen" might think least deserve it—runs throughout Luke's two-volume work.

Luke's continuation of the story from his Gospel into Acts suggests that he wants to relate the two closely—the one focusing on what Jesus began, the other on what his followers continued. Hence, the creation of the church is bound together with the story of Jesus as a significant part of the message of the gospel. The effect is twofold. On the one hand, it provides a strong argument for the certainty of the message of salvation (see Lk 1:1-4) and its effectiveness as seen in terms of the new community. On the other hand, it demonstrates the unassailable continuity between God's action in Jesus' ministry and in the Christian community. In other words, the Christian church is thus presented as the rightful heir of the salvation promised to Israel.

Conclusion

Paul has long been considered the great theologian of the apostolic church. We are beginning to realize that the writers of the Gospels and Acts have a claim to that title, too. Matthew, Mark, Luke and John are theologians—even if they have exercised their role differently than Paul or, say, the writer of the letter to the Hebrews. By telling the story they do the work of a theologian, directing light from the one gospel in various ways so that its brilliance falls on new situations and specific contexts. Because of their work, our understanding of the good news is much richer.

PART III

The Message of the Gospels

7
The Gospels
as
Story

When Mark wrote his Gospel, he created a kind of literature, a genre, for which there were few antecedents. In doing so, however, he made use of a whole host of literary forms. In addition to reading the Gospels as units, then, serious readers need to be able to discern and interpret the various ingredients which together make up each Gospel. In this chapter and the next, I propose to deal individually with the main literary forms used by the Gospel writers. Because of its pervasiveness in the Gospels and Acts, we will devote these pages to a relatively lengthy discussion of *narrative*.

Like modern writers, the evangelists were not simply out to tell a good story. They used a literary form, narrative, to communicate their message, to teach their readers. In the case of the Gospels and Acts, we must speak of "narrative" on two different levels. I have repeatedly spoken of the Gospels as stories and, despite their sometimes fragmented appearance, this is true. Hence, each Gospel—and in the case of Luke, the Gospel and Acts together—should be approached as a literary whole, with due attention paid to its overall structure and narrative progression. On the other hand, a chief ingredient of the "Gospel narrative" is the smaller narrative unit. That is, many stories combine to make up the Gospel story. In what follows, then, we will first discuss the Gospels and Acts as narrative and then discuss narrative in the Gospels and Acts.

The Gospels and Acts as Narrative

The first point modern readers of the Gospels and Acts must grasp concerns the perspective from which the evangelists explained the events they narrated. Like the writers of narrative in the Old Testament and intertestamental Judaism, the evangelists believed in *dual causation*. By this we mean that, for them, seemingly mundane events could be explained as the simple outworking of natural causes, but at the same time represented the activity of God.

Perhaps no better example of this can be found than the events of Jesus' passion. On one level Jesus' death was no doubt the result of human actions. The religious leaders conspired against him with Judas, his disciple; he betrayed Jesus into their hands; they, in turn, delivered him over to Pilate; he handed Jesus over to the soldiers, who carried out the death sentence. By the agency of a long line of humans, Jesus was crucified.

Yet the Gospels and Acts are equally clear that God was an active agent in Jesus' death. To say that the "Son of Man must suffer" (Mk 8:31) is to insist that *God's* will is carried out in Jesus' passion. While Judas must bear full responsibility for his act of betrayal, "the Son of Man will go as it has been decreed [by God himself!]" (Lk 22:22). In the narrative of Acts, Paul maintains that "in executing Jesus the people of Jerusalem and their leaders" were only carrying "out all that had been written about him" (Acts 13:26-31).

This interpretive element is an integral part of the Gospels and Acts, and modern readers must not overlook it or deny it. Obviously, the evangelists believed that in his work and words, Jesus was carrying out the will of God, foretold in the Scriptures. Likewise, Luke believed that the progress of the early church was the outworking of God's redemptive plan. In order to fully appreciate the message of these narratives, we must enter into their world and adopt their perspective, their belief that God is at work here.

Second, in interpreting the Gospels and Acts as narratives, it is vital that we see them as just that—narratives. Modern readers of the Bible often give way to a tendency to read a passage here, a text there, and think they are in this way encountering the Word of God. Even the more ambitious who sit down to read a whole Gospel often do so only a chapter or two at a time. This is better, but we must also realize that the Gospels and Acts were not written to be read in so fragmented a way. They are literary units—relatively short ones at that—and it is best to read each in one sitting.

By following this approach, we begin to understand the *overall structure and progression of the story*. We begin to get a feel for the movement of the narrative, discerning the flow of the story *as a story*. We begin to understand the structure the author himself imposed on the story. We begin to recognize the devices the author himself has used to draw the reader along and to make his point.

For example, this kind of reading of the Gospel of Mark might reveal the significance of the repeated predictions of and anticipatory allusions to Jesus' death and resurrection. Even before Jesus himself explicitly predicts his suffering death and resurrection in Mark 8:31, these events are anticipated in a variety of ways.

In Mark 2:19-20 Jesus implicitly identifies himself with the bridegroom who will be "taken away" unexpectedly. Mark 3:6 serves as the climax of the string of loosely connected stories beginning in Mark 2:1 and, in fact, is a critical point in the whole Gospel. Here, for the first time, the religious and political leaders explicitly oppose and plot against him. In Mark 6:4, Jesus identifies his fate with that of the prophets—which, according to Old Testament tradition and the religious thought of the day, entailed rejection, suffering and death. More allusions to Jesus' death may be found in Mark's Gospel, but already the point is clear. By means of the literary device of prediction and anticipation, Mark consistently draws our attention to the inevitability of Jesus' death.

Two additional, brief illustrations of how we might be attentive to narrative structure may prove helpful. First, a deliberate reading of the whole Gospel of Matthew might reveal that on five different occasions the writer has employed a stereotypical formula: "And it happened when Jesus finished . . ." (Mt 7:28; 11:1; 13:53; 19:1; 26:1). In each case, this phrase serves to draw to a close a major discourse of Jesus, drawing attention to Jesus' status as the Messiah. This is certainly important to our understanding of the flow of Matthew's narrative.

Second, we may note that in at least one case, the evangelist actually provides us with the key to his narrative structure: "But you will receive power when the Holy Spirit comes on you; and you will be my witnesses in Jerusalem, and in all Judea and Samaria, and to the ends of the earth" (Acts 1:8 NIV). In this introductory section to the Acts of the Apostles, where Luke is concerned to interweave as smoothly as possible his two books, he has actually set forth the program for his narrative.

In reading the Gospels and Acts as narrative we may note a third major suggestion. We must take seriously the authors' *selection and arrangement of material.* We have already noted that the evangelists were limited in their purpose and therefore selective of the material they would include in their narrative. In taking this seriously, we are in a sense working backwards, asking what they wanted to communicate by using *this* material.

A prime example of this can be seen in the decision of the first and third evangelists to narrate the various events surrounding Jesus' birth in their Gospels. By doing so, they indicate the significance of this event for the gospel and demonstrate that Jesus' Sonship must be traced back to his birth. Similarly, it is equally clear that Luke has included only a part of the story of the early church in his second volume. He has centered his narrative especially on Peter, then Paul, and largely excluded the work of other early missionaries and the founding of other churches. In this and other ways, Luke fails to provide us the *whole* story of the development of the early Christian mission. We must not fault him for doing so, but must recognize that he has done so quite intentionally.

Similarly, the way in which materials are arranged and the way stories are told can reveal something of the author's intent. For example, stories are often told in parallel fashion in order to make an interpretive point—as in Acts 3:1-10 and 14:8-10. The first is the story of Peter healing a lame man; the second, of Paul doing the same. Notice these parallels:

1. The man was crippled from birth. (Acts 3:2; 14:8)
2. Peter/Paul looked directly at him. (Acts 3:4; 14:9)
3. The man was attentive to Peter/Paul. (Acts 3:5; 14:9)
4. The man jumped up and walked. (Acts 3:7; 14:10)

Moreover, in each instance the healing episode gave the follower of Jesus the opportunity to preach. Why has Luke told the story in this way, actually employing identical Greek phrases in each?

Apparently, Luke is interested in drawing significant parallels between Peter and Paul. This legitimizes Paul's call to service and his ministry, and shows that the mission is developing smoothly, according to God's plan. Often, then, the way a story is told, keeping in mind the broader purposes of the evangelist, can be of significance for the attentive reader.

Narrative in the Gospels

The principles for interpreting the stories of the Gospels are not unique to the Gospels. For the purpose of illustration, however, it will help to bracket out the Acts of the Apostles for the moment. Here we will discuss five principles for interpreting narratives in the Gospels.

First, we must reiterate that all stories are by nature selective and incomplete. No writer—ancient or modern—tells everything. This observation is important, however obvious it might seem, because the corollary to this is that what does appear in the story is what the author thought was important for readers to know. For this reason, we must not engage in unbridled speculation but rather take seriously what points are narrated.

Thus, when someone tells us that Zacchaeus, the chief tax collector (Lk 19:1-10), had heard of Jesus' association with persons such as himself, we must ask, How can we know? And, if this is so, and if it is important, why does Luke not tell us? What was of obvious importance for Luke is that Zacchaeus was both a tax collector (and so despised by the church folk of his day) and a wealthy man (and so, in Luke's Gospel, a man tempted to deny his need before God). Yet he was receptive of Jesus ("he welcomed him gladly"), he repented, and he took up the cause of the poor. What was the evangelist interested in? The clue is often in the details he does include.

Second, and closely related, the stories of the Gospels were not written to answer *our* questions. In the twentieth century we have our own questions to ask and some reflect developments in fields like psychology, physiology and sociology which were largely unknown to the biblical writers. We must remember when reading the Gospels that these stories were told *by* people who had their own agenda, *for* people with particular needs. For example, modern commentators are forever trying to determine how Jesus could have fed the thousands with only one picnic lunch. However, to the evangelists it really does not matter *how* Jesus did so. For them the issue is *what* that story communicates about Jesus.

Third, stories are not to be regarded as allegories, in which a hidden, esoteric meaning is couched in every detail and personality. Often, in fact, a story is told to make only one central point. To consider how this happens, we may introduce a further principle.

Fourth, narratives often teach indirectly or illustratively. Many Christians have been taught that narratives are simply to be taken at face value; they are not theological in character. This approach has led to greater pedagogical value being placed on writings like the Pauline letters or the epistle of James which, it is presumed, teach the truth of God clearly. This point of view fails to take seriously the reality we have stressed again and again—namely, the evangelists intended to relate the gospel to the lives of their audiences, and in doing so they told a story.

Narrative and epistle—both are simply alternative ways in which to communicate a message. While I shall introduce a safeguard in the last point below about how narrative teaches, my point here is that the stories told by the evangelists do intend to communicate truth, however indirectly. In seeking to understand the Gospel stories, we will want to pay special attention to the following:

1. Who? What? Where? When? Why? By way of inquiring into the message of the narrative, we may start with the obvious—the famed journalistic questions. The stories of the Gospels are consistently self-contained, with the narrative flow fairly obvious, and these questions will help us at the initial stage of interpretation.

2. The length of the narrative is sometimes important. Unlike some modern writers, those early evangelists never contemplated the possibility of writing a seemingly endless story. Because of the nature of the available writing materials, they faced the limits of space in a way we cannot fully imagine. For this reason, we are justified in calling attention to the idea that the relative length of a narrative provides a hint as to its importance and meaning.

For example, we may justifiably ask why Mark, whose interest is in the story of Jesus, expends so much valuable space telling the story of the death of John the Baptist (Mk 6:14-29). One answer is clear: Mark uses this story as another in a long line of predictions and allusions to Jesus' own disastrous fate. At the same time, John's faithfulness and fate illustrate the cost of discipleship, another theme of significance for Mark.

Similarly, the length of the Cornelius narrative in Acts 10:1-11:18 is an indication of its significance for Luke. Apparently, he regarded the spread of the gospel to Gentiles as a major turning point for the early Christian mission. By telling the story in such detail—and even repeating its main outline almost immediately, he expresses the undeniable fact that *God's* purpose is to grant salvation to the Gentiles (see Acts 11:18), and so he prepares his readers for the more brief account of the first Gentile church at Antioch (Acts 11:19-26).

3. The positioning of the story itself often holds a clue to its interpretation. In chapter four, we saw how the placement of

the story of the temple-cleansing in John's Gospel affected the way it should be understood.

A particularly interesting placement device found in the Gospels, especially in Mark, is known as *intercalation*. This device, also referred to as "sandwiching," involves one story framing another. In Mark 11:12-21, for example, the story of cursing the fig tree frames the story of cleansing the temple. In this way, Mark interprets the *cleansing* of the temple as *cursing* the temple. The time of the temple has finished; it will be replaced by Jesus himself. In John 18:15-27, the story of Jesus' trial by the Jewish authorities is sandwiched between the two parts of the story of Peter's denial of Jesus. In this way, the faithfulness of Jesus is emphasized over against Peter's weakness, and Christians are encouraged to follow the example of Jesus (see 1 Tim 6:13).

4. Readers of the Gospels must also be on the lookout for interpretive statements built into the story itself, often appearing as the climax of the narrative. Returning to the Zacchaeus episode, we note that at the end of this story we hear Jesus making an important self-statement: "For the Son of Man came to seek and to save the lost" (Lk 19:10). In this way, we discover the true significance of the preceding story: it embodies and illustrates the character of the mission of the Son of Man. Likewise, Mark 2:1-12 relates how Jesus heals a paralytic, but the true significance of the story rests in its ability to communicate the authority of the Son of Man to forgive sins (Mk 2:10).

5. Another interpretive device built into the narrative is the editorial comment which links one story to another. After Jesus walks on the water in Mark 6:45-50, the disciples are completely amazed. Why? Mark tells us: "they had not understood about the loaves; their hearts were hardened" (Mk 6:52). In this way Mark draws the reader back to the preceding story, where Jesus feeds the five thousand (Mk 6:30-44). He deliberately relates the one story to the other in order to communicate the message.

Thus we have drawn attention to a sampling of principles which, when applied, will help us come to terms with the message of the stories which make up the Gospels. In employing these and other points of approach, we must realize the importance of allowing the narrative to speak to us, the readers. The story itself often contains all we need to understand it.

Fifth, and last, while recognizing that the narrative is but one more way in which theological and historical interests can be communicated, we must also be clear about an important limitation of the narrative genre. Stories are *not* propositional statements about what must happen in every instance. The details of a narrative must not be drafted into service to outline how God will or must always operate. In his helpful little book, *Let's Quit Fighting about the Holy Spirit,* Peter E. Gillquist tells a story which effectively illustrates this danger.

It's late in the second year of Jesus' public ministry, and He is teaching a group of His followers on a Judean hillside. Among those in the crowd are two men who have not met before and who happen to be seated next to each other.

While the Lord is revealing the things of God to the throng, the one man nudges the other and remarks, "Isn't He wonderful?"

"He certainly is," whispers the second. "He healed me of blindness, you know."

"He did!" says the first with surprise. "He healed me of blindness, too!"

"That's amazing," the second man remarks, motioning to his new friend to pull away from the crowd a bit so their talking will not cause disturbance. "How did it happen?"

"Well, this friend of mine—who was also blind—and I were sitting by the edge of the road just outside of Jericho. We could tell from the voices of an approaching crowd that the Lord was coming our way and would soon pass us on the road.

"When he was within earshot, we yelled up to Him something like, 'Oh Lord, Son of David, give us Your mercy.'

"Jesus called over to us and said, 'What do you want Me to do for you?'

"We said, 'Lord, we just want to be able to see.' And in a flash, we both had our eyesight restored."

"Wait a minute!" says the second man, with a note of contempt in his voice. "There's no way it could have happened like that."

"What are you talking about?" replies the first.

"You've got to have *mud,*" says the other. "See, first you spit into your hands, then you stoop down and get some dirt, and go to a pool and wash the mud from your . . ."

And there you have it, folks. The start of the world's first two denominations. The Mudites and the Anti-Mudites.[1]
This rather humorous illustration of our point should not be allowed to mask its seriousness. Narratives do not inform the readers of the Gospels what ought to happen every time.

Narrative in the Acts of the Apostles
I do not intend to begin listing additional principles for interpreting the narratives in the Acts of the Apostles. As I mentioned before, many of the same ideas discussed in the previous section are equally useful in a reading of Acts. Instead, I propose to illustrate this approach with a look at one important, controversial narrative—the Pentecost story in Acts 2. In doing so, I hope to follow the flow of the narrative, suggest the significance of the story for Luke and remark on the significance of this narrative for our own day.[2]

1. A debated story. This narrated event has been the focus of some debate among Christians attempting to outline a coherent, univocal theology of the Holy Spirit. Some, for example, would have us believe that the outpouring of the Holy Spirit in Acts 2 is a definite example of a "second blessing." According to this interpretation, the account of John 20:21-22 is adduced as proof that the disciples were already "saved," and so Pentecost is regarded as a subsequent reception of the Spirit. The primary implication of this way of thinking is this: Christians today who claim to have committed their lives to Christ must now take the second step and seek for themselves the outpouring of the Holy Spirit.

Others look to this narrative as proof that the gift of tongues is always associated with the outpouring of the Holy Spirit.

Hence, "Spirit-filled" Christians are those who have experienced the gift of tongues.

2. *Basic method of approach.* At the very outset of our discussion, we must remember that we cannot start by trying to interpret Luke in the light of John—or, for that matter, John in the light of Luke. Our approach must begin elsewhere. We should first try to understand what Luke is trying to communicate in this passage—and indeed in his whole two-volume work. We also work to understand John's message, allowing John to be John. Only then are we in a position to allow interaction at the level of the respective messages of the texts.

This also means that we do not go to Paul to learn the significance of Pentecost; after all, Paul never even mentions the event! Nor do we necessarily allow Paul's message to speak with more authority than Luke's, simply because the one is written in epistolary prose, the other in narrative. We allow Luke to be Luke, and we allow Paul to be Paul.

3. *The narrative structure.* The flow of the narrative is easy enough to follow. The disciples had been waiting in Jerusalem at Jesus' command (Acts 1:4), and on the day of Pentecost what had been promised came to pass. In the midst of various exceptional phenomena, the Holy Spirit is poured out on the disciples who then are "filled with the Holy Spirit." In association with this "filling," they begin to speak in unknown tongues—an occurrence which is given two interpretations in the narrative.

First, the crowd is astonished because they hear the wonders of God proclaimed in their own languages. This in itself is a mission event of major importance. Second, however, some saw the ecstatic speech as merely the babbling of drunken men and women. This gives Peter the opportunity he needs to address the crowd, and he does so, insisting that what was taking place was not the fruit of too much wine. Instead, it was the fulfillment of prophecy. Quoting Joel 2:28-32, Peter then goes on to proclaim the salvation of the Lord, after which some three thousand become disciples.

The narrative thus emphasizes the mission of the disciples

brought about by the outpouring of the Holy Spirit, who added greatly to their numbers.

4. The significance of the Pentecost story for Luke. Two points suggest that the Pentecost story is of monumental consequence for Luke. On the one hand, we have only to look at the length of this tale. On the other, we may note its position in the book of Acts. The first chapter of Acts is certainly important: it bridges the gap between the Gospel of Luke and the Acts of the Apostles (the introductory verses, the ascension story and the choosing of a twelfth disciple) and relates something of the agenda of the whole narrative (1:8). However, most of the emphasis falls on the Pentecost story—which itself fulfills Jesus' promise in Luke 24:49 and Acts 1:4, 8. Here, at the beginning of the narrative of the Christian mission, is the story which sets the stage for and determines the contours of the events to follow in the rest of the book.

In pointing out more particularly the significance of the story for Luke, we may outline the following:

First, Pentecost is clearly the climax of all that has gone on before. The outpouring of the Spirit is the fulfillment of the prophecy of John the Baptist (Lk 3:15-17) and of Jesus himself (Lk 24:49; Acts 1:4-5). The earlier narrative has anticipated this event which, along with Jesus' ascension, is regarded as the climax of Jesus' ministry: "Exalted to the right hand of God, he has received from the Father the promised Holy Spirit and has poured out what you now see and hear" (Acts 2:33 NIV). Moreover, Pentecost is the fulfillment of Scripture (Joel 2:28-32; see Acts 2:17-21). With the outpouring of the Holy Spirit, the time has come when "everyone who calls on the name of the Lord will be saved" (Acts 2:21 NIV).

Second, not only is Pentecost the climax of what has gone on before, it is also the beginning of something new. Pentecost marks the birth of the church, and with it, its universal, Spirit-empowered mission.

Third, the narrative is constructed such that the primary focus falls on the universal mission of the church. "The gift of the Spirit equips the disciples for witness, Peter's proclamation of the gospel occupies the centre of the account, and the story culminates in the conversion of some 3,000 hearers of the message."[3]

5. *The story of Pentecost today*. What, then, is the abiding significance of this narrative for us today? First, we may note that Pentecost is a nonrepeatable event. Only once can the new age be ushered in and the church be given birth. We should not, therefore, try to read our experience back into that account, nor expect that the events of Pentecost constitute some sort of pattern for today's church. This is not to say, however, that we may glean nothing from this story for ourselves. Indeed, while Pentecost itself cannot be repeated, the story makes clear that the reception of the Spirit can and should be repeated (Acts 2:33, 38).

Why does the Spirit come? If we learn anything from this story, it is certainly that the gift of the Spirit determines and regulates the mission of the Christian community.[4] Pentecost and mission are inseparable in this narrative. The whole of the Acts of the Apostles demonstrates that this is equally true for the expansion of the early church. Where the Spirit is poured out, there is the church involved in mission.

Conclusion

More than anything else, the Gospels and Acts are story. For this reason some readers of the New Testament may regard them as less theological than, say, Paul's letter to the Philippians. To the contrary, I have tried to indicate that a great deal about the redemptive work of God is embedded in these narratives. Moreover, I have provided some ideas and guidelines for taking seriously the theological importance of the Gospels and Acts as story. We have discovered that with attentive reading we allow the story to unfold its own drama and confront us with its own message.

8
Story-Telling in the Gospels

Narrative may be the primary genre employed by the Gospel writers, but it is certainly not the only one. A variety of literary forms are integrated into the Gospels and Acts, all with their own ways of communicating the message of the gospel. In this chapter we will continue to discuss individually some of the main literary forms adopted by the evangelists. Gospels research in this century has recognized a number of literary forms in the Gospels, but we will focus on only a few where interpretive hints are especially needed.

The Genealogy
Both Matthew and Luke employ genealogical tables in their Gospels. Often regarded as the most boring and least edifying segments of the Bible, genealogies actually serve important theological functions. Their potential contribution can be illustrated through a careful reading of the genealogy of Jesus in Matthew 1:1-17.[1] This ancestral list contains certain irregularities. Once recognized, they point toward a more complete understanding of the role of Matthew's genealogy in particular and of biblical genealogies more broadly.

1. Rather than simply record Jesus' family record, Matthew establishes at the very beginning Jesus' relation to two outstanding persons: he is the son of David and the son of Abraham (Mt 1:1). Similarly in the introduction to this genealogy Matthew refers to Jesus, the *Christ*. The phrase "Son of David" occurs frequently in the Gospel of Matthew and was known for its messianic significance by Paul as well (see Rom 1:3). In designating Jesus as a descendent of David, Matthew calls to mind God's promise to David: "I will raise up your offspring to succeed you . . . and I will establish his kingdom" (2 Sam 7:12 NIV). By referring to Jesus as a descendant of Abraham, Matthew recalls God's promise to Abraham that in his offspring all nations would be blessed (Gen 22:18; compare Gal 3:15-18).

Already, then, before the list of Jesus' ancestors commences, we recognize that Matthew is not including this genealogy simply for historical purposes. He has a theological point to make; he wants to relate Jesus' birth directly with God's work of salvation in the past and future.

2. We are rightly shocked by the inclusion of women in this list of Jesus' ancestors. To be called a "son of your mother" (rather than "of your father") was an insult (see Mk 6:3), and in any case, in this ancient culture purity of descent was not demonstrated through female ancestors. What is more, none of these women were above reproach.

Tamar was a Canaanite who seduced Judah, her father-in-law (Gen 38). *Rahab* was a non-Israelite, too, and a prostitute (Josh 2). *Ruth* was a foreigner, a Moabitess (Ruth)—and so was impure (see Deut 23:3). Moreover, her union with Boaz was irregular, if not scandalous. *Bathsheba* (the wife of Uriah) is best remembered for her sexual misdeeds with King David (2 Sam 11).

Why did Matthew include women—and especially *these* women—in his record of Jesus' ancestors? The most plausible answer is that they illustrate God's readiness to use very surprising circumstances to accomplish his redemptive purpose. The presence of these women thus prepares us for an even more surprising event, the virgin birth of Jesus (Mt 1:18). One thing is clear: in including women with scandalous reputations in this genealogy, Matthew again demonstrates that he is not attempting to record a strict chronology of Jesus' ancestors.

3. If Matthew intended to give us a precise family record, he has made some surprising omissions: Ahaziah, Jehoash and Amaziah should have been included after Joram in verse 8, and the name of Jehoiakim should have appeared after Josiah in verse 11. (Josiah was the *grandfather* of Jeconiah—whom Matthew lists here.)[2]

Why these omissions? Apparently, the evangelist has been guided by his interest in documenting the pattern of Israel's history in three groups of fourteen generations—from Abraham to David, David to the exile, and the exile to Christ (Mt 1:17). People today may find this a problem because of our penchant for detailed accuracy, but we must not read our concerns into Matthew. Omissions of this nature were not uncommon in the ancient world. As Robert Mounce observes, "the somewhat rough genealogical table serves Matthew's purpose of setting forth the royal and messianic ancestry of Jesus of Nazareth."[3]

4. Finally, we must note Matthew's surprising arithmetic. In verse 17 he informs us that Jesus' ancestry embraces three groups of fourteen generations (3 x 14). The first section lists fourteen generations, beginning with Abraham and ending with David. The second group lists fourteen more generations through to Jeconiah. The third group, however, lists only thirteen additional generations through to Jesus. Numerous attempts to solve this riddle have been made, but we are left with the impression that Matthew was much more interested in claiming his 3 x 14 pattern of generations for Jesus' genealogy than in working out that pattern in his list for his readers. The writings of Matthew's contemporaries often demonstrate an interest in the symbolic use of numbers and patterns—which, then, need not always be interpreted woodenly. No doubt, Matthew was interested in making a theological point with this arithmetic.[4]

Our observations suggest that Matthew's genealogy should

be understood *theologically,* for Matthew himself intends it so. By the use of the genealogical form, he communicates that Jesus is the Messiah. In fact, genealogies (like other literary forms—narrative, poetry, and so forth) are often employed in Scripture to express apologetic, theological and nationalistic concerns. Their message entails far more than historical data.

The Apocalyptic Discourse
The Gospels were written well within the period commonly associated with the drafting of apocalyptic literature, 250 B.C. to A.D. 150.[5] *Apocalyptic* signifies "revelatory," and, characteristically, literature of this nature discloses a hidden message in the form of a narrative. Ordinarily, the message thus revealed anticipates God's climactic redemptive action at the end of time, while interpreting present, earthly events and persons in other-worldly or supernatural categories.

Of course, the Gospels are not themselves apocalyptic literature, though certain themes stressed in apocalyptic (for example, the resurrection) are prominent.[6] The most significant use of apocalyptic literary forms in the Gospels is in Mark 13 and its parallels, Matthew 24 and Luke 21. Each of these is appropriately called an apocalyptic discourse.

By way of comparison, here is a similar discourse from 4 Ezra 6:18-28:

Behold, the days are coming, and it shall be that when I draw near to visit the inhabitants of the earth, and when I require from the doers of iniquity the penalty of their iniquity, and when the humiliation of Zion is complete, and when the seal is placed upon the age which is about to pass away, then I will show these signs: The books shall be opened before the firmament, and all shall see it together. Infants a year old shall speak with their voices, and women with child shall give birth to premature children at three or four months, and these shall live and dance. Sown places shall suddenly appear unsown, and full storehouses shall suddenly be found to be empty; and the trumpet shall sound aloud, and when all hear it, they shall suddenly be terrified. At that time friends shall make war on friends like enemies, and the earth and those who inhabit it shall be terrified, and the springs of the fountains shall stand still, so that for three hours they shall not flow.

It shall be that whoever remains after all that I have fore-told to you shall be saved and shall see my salvation and the end of my world. And they shall see the men who were taken up, who from their birth have not tasted death; and the heart of the earth's inhabitants shall be changed and converted to a different spirit. For evil shall be blotted out, and deceit shall be quenched; faithfulness shall flourish, and corruption shall be overcome, and the truth, which has been so long without fruit, shall be revealed.[7]

As this example illustrates, apocalyptic discourses are note-worthy for their description of the catastrophes which will char-acterize the time before the end, after which God himself will intervene in a dramatic and decisive way. Often a description of the judgment will follow—with emphasis on the damnation of the unjust and salvation of the righteous. That the discourse of Mark 13 fits this general pattern is clear, though the scene of judgment is even more evident in Matthew 24—25.

Moreover, as in this example, such discourses characteristi-cally draw their content from two primary sources—the Scrip-tures and the experience of the writer and his community. The Scriptures serve as raw material both as an arsenal from which to choose specific texts and as a language-bank from which to draw scriptural allusions.[8] The apocalyptic discourse of Mark 13 is no exception to this, and allusions to the Old Testament are especially transparent at two crucial junctures. First, in Mark 13:14, the desecration of the temple is spoken of in terms bor-rowed from Daniel 9:27, 11:31 and 12:11. Second, in Mark 13:24-26, the coming of the Son of Man is prepared for with a scriptural conglomerate from Isaiah 13:10, 34:4, Joel 2:10 and 31, and is described in the words of Daniel 7:13.

As obvious as the generic relationship between Mark 13 and similar Jewish apocalyptic discourses is, there is a key differ-ence. Unlike its close counterparts, the discourse related in

Mark 13 does not intend to provide esoteric information about the end. There is no attempt here to provide persons with a calendar for end-time events.

Two *structural* observations demonstrate this truth. First, verses 5-31 do not constitute an answer to the question of the disciples in Mark 13:4 ("Tell us, when will these things [that is, the end] take place?"). That answer comes finally in verse 32: "No one knows about that day or hour, not even the angels in heaven, nor the Son, but only the Father." In other apocalyptic discourses, a mediator of divine truth might be quite prepared to dispense such information, but not Jesus. He goes so far as to declare his own ignorance on the subject.

Second, the whole discourse is peppered with instruction and encouragement regarding faithfulness:

Watch out that no one deceives you. (v. 5)

You must *be on your guard.* (v. 9)

So *be on your guard;* I have told you everything ahead of time. (v. 23)

Be on guard! Be alert! (v. 33)

And, finally, at the climax of the discourse, a parable is told, the message of which is crystal clear: "What I say to you, I say to everyone, 'Watch!' " (v. 37). The didactic cutting edge of this whole discourse is self-evident.[9]

This programmatic emphasis is therefore the key to making sense of the apocalyptic discourse-material of the Gospels. The stress falls on the role of Jesus as the Lord of history (see especially Mk 13:23), thus on strengthening the faith of the readers of the Gospels. Believers, then, are not encouraged to speculate about the end times, but are urged to "be ready!"

As with all apocalyptic literature, the apocalyptic discourse is more interested in painting pictures and inspiring the imagination of faith, and less interested in describing detailed events with any degree of precision.[10] Hence the futuristic and fantastic contents of the discourse must not be read woodenly, as though precise, point-for-point historical referents must be found for each image. Rather they are symbols that point to material, social and political conditions in the present age—

that is, the last days, the era between Jesus' resurrection and his return—when all Christians must maintain constant readiness.

The Farewell Discourse

In the literature of the ancient world it was not uncommon to include speeches from dying or departing persons.[11] This is true in the Greco-Roman world as well as in the Old Testament. Examples of the farewell discourse in the Hebrew Scriptures may be found in Genesis 47:29—50:14, Joshua 23:1—24:32, 1 Samuel 12 and other texts.

It is not extraordinary, then, that farewell speeches are also included in the Gospels and Acts. Among the former are the discourses associated with Jesus' last meal in Luke and John. In Acts 20:17-38 we read of Paul's farewell speech delivered to the leaders of the church at Ephesus. Elements of the farewell discourse are also associated with the stories of Jesus' resurrection appearances in the Gospels—as seen particularly in Jesus' commissioning of the disciples to carry on the ministry he himself had begun.

The Last Supper and related "table talk" is narrated by Luke in 22:14-38. As a part of the meal itself, we read of Jesus' awareness of his impending death and of his own interpretation of his death (vv. 15-20). In predicting not only his suffering but also the coming of the kingdom, Jesus provides a basis for future hope even in this sorrowful context. Afterwards, Jesus issues a series of warnings and encouragements related to the near and distant future. He briefly reminisces about his own trials and mentions his intercession on behalf of Peter, but devotes the bulk of this last discourse to a series of prophecies and warnings related to his disciples' future (vv. 21-38). The structure of this speech is not unlike what we might expect in a farewell discourse.

In John's Gospel, however, we find two interesting, divergent points worthy of mention. First, we read not one, but two or three "farewell discourses" which have been placed side by side (Jn 13:1—17:26). John 14:31 definitely marks the end of the first, for there Jesus himself declares, "Come now; let us leave."

More peculiar in the context of the farewell speech, however, is the extended prayer of Jesus in John 17. Prayers of this nature are not common in this context, though we may recall that Luke had already noted Jesus' assertion that he would intercede on behalf of Peter (Lk 22:32). Then, too, Paul prays with the Ephesian elders at the close of his speech of departure recorded in Acts 20:36.

In order to properly understand the farewell discourse, two things must be remembered. First, we must recall the context in which these words are recorded. The farewell discourse acquires its social gravity and poignancy especially from the situation in which it is delivered. Second, and closely related, we must take into account the *purpose* of the discourse. In the Greco-Roman world, such a speech was often employed to cite the heroic character and courageous exploits of the departing one. Not so in the Gospels and Acts! In these contexts, the spotlight falls not on hero worship, but on preparation for the future. Jesus instructs his disciples in order that they will be able to stand firm in the midst of the coming struggle, so that they will not lose hope when he is gone. The farewell discourse is an extended "word of encouragement."

Of course, in Acts 20 we find Paul reminiscing about his ministry among the Ephesians, but even there the purpose is not self-glorification. Rather, as in his letters, Paul appeals to his own example as a means for encouraging and instructing others. His primary intent, then, is to exhort the Ephesian leaders to faithfully assume pastoral care for the brothers and sisters in their Christian fellowship.

Sayings of Jesus

Our main discussion of the method of Jesus' teaching will come in chapters nine and ten. Not all of the points of interpretive importance are easily covered in those sections, however, and so we will make a few preliminary observations here.

1. Sayings in context. Regardless of the form of speech Jesus chooses, his sayings must not be isolated from their contexts. This is true for sayings of all kinds, even those which appear to be independent of surrounding material.

For example, the reader of the Third Gospel might seem totally unprepared for the saying about salt in Luke 14:34: "Salt is good, but if it loses its saltiness, how can it be made salty again? It is fit neither for the soil nor for the manure pile; it is thrown out" (NIV). Its introduction into this section on the cost of discipleship (14:25-35) appears abrupt, and we might therefore conclude that it must be read on its own. In fact, isolated from its context in Luke this little saying communicates a well-known idea.

Serious readers of the Gospels, however, would do well to ask, Why here? Why has Luke placed this text in *this* context and not some other which might make more sense to us? If we ask this question, then we are forced to inquire into the possible relation of this short saying to the surrounding material. As it turns out, the salt-saying is related to the preceding discussion of the cost of discipleship after all. In this context, it suggests the ultimate uselessness of the disciple whose commitment is not absolute.

In stories in which sayings appear, it is likewise necessary to pay attention to context. In such instances, the saying often acts something like a punch line, interpreting the meaning of the narrated event.

Even extended discourses or collections of sayings must be read in context. We have seen the necessity of doing this in the case of the farewell discourse. This is also true for other lengthy "sermons," where the interpreter is encouraged to look for patterns, logic, structure and purpose *within* the sermon itself, *and* to inquire into the function of the sermon in the context of the whole Gospel.

This need is nowhere more transparent than in the Sermon on the Mount, recorded in Matthew 5—7. While this is only one of a number of extended discourses in the Gospels, this one has attracted the most attention in Christian circles. Indeed, it has often been sundered from its context in Matthew and treated as a "compendium of Christian ethics."[12] In fact, this sermon is well integrated into the structure and theology of the First

Gospel, laying important groundwork especially in the areas of Christology, eschatology, discipleship and Christian community. Hence, a reading which does justice to the intent of the evangelist must take seriously the role of the Sermon in the whole Gospel.

In the final analysis, I am only insisting that the evangelists included the material they have in the locations they have *for a reason.* Hence, the sayings of Jesus are properly read *in context.*

2. *Characteristic speech of Jesus.* Jesus employs three special expressions which, because of their unusual nature, call for special attention. The first is the phrase with which he often introduces his statements: "Amen, I say to you . . ." *Amen* is a Hebrew word signifying something like "certainly"; hence, many modern translations render it as "truly." In the Gospels, however, Jesus uses it without exception to introduce his own words. What did it signify? The formula we noted above has its only real analogy in the prophetic expression used in the Old Testament: "Thus says the Lord . . ." With this expression, the prophets made clear to their audiences that what they were saying was not based on their authority but on the Lord's. Jesus' expression must be contrasted with the prophetic appeal to the authority of the Lord. What he says is based on his *own* authority.[13]

Second, Jesus addresses God with the Aramaic word *Abba,* which signified a claim of intimacy with God which was unusual in Jesus' day.[14] By addressing God in this way, Jesus was claiming for himself an unusually intimate bond with God.

Third, the favorite expression by which Jesus refers to himself is the problematic phrase "Son of Man."[15] Many contemporary Christians regard "Son of Man" as a statement about Jesus' *humanity,* in distinction from the apparent reference to his *divinity* in the title "Son of God." This notion is far from the truth. The debate regarding how Jesus would have understood this term is a heated one, but there can be no question that in the Gospels "Son of Man" is an honorific title, by which Jesus claims for himself the divine status associated with the Son of Man figure in Daniel 7. As the Son of Man, Jesus lived his life as a servant, gave his life for the salvation of the world and was raised from the dead. He thus created and gathered a new people of God and will return in power to consummate his work, instituting in a definitive and final way the reign of God.

The Speeches of Acts

One of the more prominent aspects of the Acts narrative is the abundance of speeches. This is true both in terms of the large amount of space allotted them, and in their status as theological documents. Many scholars, past and present, have argued that these speeches are Luke's creations and are therefore not to be associated with the history of earliest Christianity.

Of course, we can hardly argue that they are historical in the strictest sense of the term. After all, Luke lacked the technological capacity to record those sermons on tape and have them transcribed word for word. In Acts 2:40 he tells his readers quite clearly that he is providing only a summary. Moreover, there can be no denying that Luke has indeed given these speeches in his own words and style.[16] However, it is one thing to admit that Luke has had a hand in the composition of these speeches, but quite another thing to suppose he is totally responsible for their content.[17]

In fact, several lines of evidence point to Luke's use of tradition in the sermons in Acts. For example, only once in this whole book does the subject of justification by faith raise its head, and that in a sermon attributed to Paul (Acts 13:39). Then, too, there are many parallels between the theology of the sermons attributed to Peter and the first letter that bears his name. And while Paul himself never tells the story of his Damascus-road experience in his letters, this experience was clearly monumentally significant for him—and this accords well with the essence of Luke's portrait.[18] More technical analyses of the sermons have turned up numerous historical reminiscences, and we can be assured that Luke has not simply created these speeches out of nothing.

The question remains, however, why Luke included these sermons at all. We may mention two main reasons. First, in doing so Luke presents us with an early church for whom preaching was of central import. If the rest of the New Testament is any indication, Luke was undoubtedly representing historical reality. Second, the speeches are of theological significance in the narrative of Acts, and in them we see something of the outline of Luke's understanding of the gospel message. By implementing this material, casting it in his own style and vocabulary, and giving it such prominence in the overall development of the story, Luke adopts its message as his own. They carry his own theology.

Broadly speaking, when we refer to the speeches in Acts we are actually calling attention to the missionary sermons and to the speeches of public defense by Stephen and Paul. The former sermons congregate in the first half of the book; the latter speeches are found mostly in the latter half, the speech of Stephen providing an exception to this generalization.

As we might expect, the purpose of each kind of speech differs. Hence, the missionary sermons divulge Luke's salvation-oriented theology, suggesting the content of the gospel and the proper response to its proclamation. Each sermon is contextually oriented so that its content is related to the intended audience and we are able to see what response was given to each. By way of illustrating this last point, note that Paul's sermons to Gentiles in Acts can hardly be recognized as specifically Christian at all. Rather, his words focus on monotheism, for this was the first step needed by non-Jewish women and men, persons not already committed to a belief in the one, true God.

The defense speeches are primarily apologetic, providing a rationale for the existence of the Christian faith over against Judaism (Acts 7) and charting the authenticity and legitimacy of Christianity within the greater Roman world.

What rules should guide our reading of the speeches in Acts? Above all, we should remember that they must be understood within their context in Luke-Acts, and not in terms of Paul's (or Peter's) theology as known to us from other sources. Paul's sermons in Acts do not purport to provide summaries of his thought. They make up a part of the interpretation of the gospel of Jesus Christ in Luke-Acts, and they are to be understood in this way.

Beyond this, one should remember to read each speech as a unit, not taking bits and pieces out of the whole to prove a point. Each has its own inner logic and structure, and this can be grasped only by studying each as a whole. Moreover, our reading of the speeches in Acts will be enhanced by careful attention to their use of the Old Testament. At times the Hebrew Scriptures seem to determine the shape of the argument. At others they provide only the proper language for speaking about God's redemptive activity. At all times, however, the Old Testament is viewed as the ultimate authority for making statements about the outworking of the gospel.

Conclusion

Genealogies, apocalyptic and farewell discourses, sayings of Jesus, and the speeches in Acts—all of these forms of literature are important examples of the variety of genres used by the evangelists. As we have learned to expect, in the hands of the writers of the Gospels and Acts each becomes a legitimate tool for communicating the message of the gospel. Each has been incorporated into the overall narrative framework for a purpose. They are used for theological, evangelistic and apologetic reasons. The task of the reader is to uncover those reasons and mine these various sections of the Gospels and Acts for their message.

9
The Form
of Jesus'
Message

What was it about Jesus that attracted people to him? The force of his personality? His anointment by the Spirit? The content of his message? How can we explain the profound impact he made on thousands of people in the first century? No simple answer exists. In truth, a number of factors must be considered—including *who* was communicating, *what* was being communicated, and *how* it was being communicated.

In this chapter and the next (where we look more closely at Jesus' parables), we will be looking into the *method* of Jesus' teaching. In taking us in this direction, I do not mean to suggest that his method of teaching alone accounts for his amazing influence and impact. Rather, I want to emphasize that the *form* in which a message is couched affects how that message should be interpreted. Thus, identifying some of the forms of Jesus' teaching will help us to understand what he had to say. Awareness of the forms of Jesus' teaching also assists us in understanding how Jesus' message has been so well preserved for us, while at the same time helping to explain why the teaching of Jesus remains something of a mystery even after hundreds of years.

In his book on *The Method and Message of Jesus' Teachings*, Robert H. Stein has devoted a lengthy chapter to the "The Form of Jesus' Teaching."[1] If you wish to pursue the discussion beyond what we can here, this is the place to go. Here we will focus more specifically on two or three devices employed by Jesus which have special significance for *interpreting* the message of the Gospels.

Figurative Language

You are the salt of the earth. (Mt 5:13 NIV)

You are the light of the world. (Mt 5:14 NIV)

These are among the most well-known expressions attributed to Jesus in the Gospels, and it is not incidental that both communicate their message through the use of figurative language. To an impressive degree, symbolic words and expressions make up the warp and woof of Jesus' message. He relies on all sorts of figurative language to help his audiences picture his sayings, as in these two examples recorded in the Third Gospel:

Can a blind man lead a blind man? Will they not both fall into a pit? (Lk 6:39 NIV)

Why do you look at the speck of sawdust in your brother's eye and pay no attention to the plank in your own eye? (Lk 6:39-40 NIV)

In both instances, through his choice of language, Jesus conjures up in the minds of his listeners pictures which embody his message.

Figurative language thus used defies "literal" interpretation as often defined. When used figuratively, "words" are not strictly synonymous with "meaning." That is, in figurative speech, words are used in ways in which the correspondence between word and meaning is not straightforward. Figurative speech appeals first to our imagination, and not to our cognitive abilities. In the examples just cited, we would be sorely mistaken to think Jesus is really concerned with the abilities of blind people or with the goings-on in sawmills. Hence, our reading of Jesus' first saying should not lead us to ask when it is possible for one blind person to lead another. Jesus is painting pictures with words, and they ought not to be understood in a literal or wooden way.

Communicators use figurative words and expressions precisely because such language carries many connotations with it. These connotations help us move from more or less familiar experiences or expressions to less common ideas. To assert "you are the salt of the earth" is to fill listeners' minds with all sorts of images. By drawing a comparison between salt (a well-known object) and disciples, Jesus is able to communicate something important about discipleship in a universally understood way. As G. B. Caird has observed, comparisons of this kind are "the main road leading from the known to the unknown."[2]

Comparisons of this nature can either occur implicitly or explicitly. *Implicit* comparisons are often referred to as metaphors. Analogies of this variety abound in the sayings of Jesus: Jesus likens his followers to light and salt, Herod to a fox, Pharisees and teachers of the law to snakes, and so on. *Explicit* comparisons are called similes, and are introduced with such comparative words as *like* or *as*. Jesus was fond of this means of comparison, too, as in the following illustrations:

Woe to you, teachers of the law and Pharisees, you hypocrites! You are *like* whitewashed tombs, which look beautiful on the outside but on the inside are full of dead men's bones and everything unclean. (Mt 23:27 NIV)

This is what the kingdom of God is *like*. A man scatters seed on the ground. Night and day, whether he sleeps or gets up, the seed sprouts and grows, though he does not know how. All by itself the soil produces grain—first the stalk, then the head, then the full kernel in the head. As soon as the grain is ripe, he puts the sickle to it, because the harvest has come. (Mk 4:26-29 NIV)

As recorded in Matthew's narrative, Jesus uses figurative language (burial imagery) to paint for us a portrait of the true condition of the Jewish leaders he is attacking. In the parable from Mark's Gospel, the character of the kingdom of God (the unknown) is explained by means of its similarity to a basic agricultural process (the known).

A special form of word-picture found in the Fourth Gospel is the collection of the seven "I am" sayings:

I am the bread of life. (6:35, 41, 48, 51)

I am the light of the world. (8:12; 9:5)

I am the door of the sheep. (10:7, 9)

I am the good shepherd. (10:11, 14)

I am the resurrection and the life. (11:25)

I am the way, the truth and the life. (14:6)

I am the true vine. (15:1, 5)

On the one hand, these sayings function very much like any other metaphor, drawing on familiar images to communicate who Jesus is. Inasmuch as Jesus refers to himself as "the bread of life" he is at least appealing to the well-known life-sustaining nature of bread. On the other hand, these sayings are much more than metaphors, for through them Jesus is making an intrinsic claim about himself.[3] He is not merely comparing himself with bread. Rather, he is placing himself over against bread. He is the bread *of life*, the bread *that comes down from heaven*, the *living* bread (Jn 6:48-58). *Unlike* natural bread, then, that bread which Jesus offers (that is, himself) ends all hunger pains for eternity.

The special class of figurative language we have just considered alerts us to an important point. When dealing with metaphors and similes, we must take care not to press the point of comparison too far. The figurative language we are considering is not to be confused with allegory, where point-for-point correspondence is expected. The use of metaphor and simile recognizes that no two things are exactly alike. Indeed, even in the most straightforward cases, analogies break down when pushed too far. What is the point of comparison intended by the speaker? This is the question to be answered by readers of the Gospels, and sufficient evidence for a reasonable response can generally be gained from careful attention to context.[4]

Exaggeration

Another means Jesus uses to grab the attention of his listeners is exaggeration. Like the parent who says to the wayward child, "I've told you a million times not to do such and such," Jesus sometimes overstates his case in order to make his point. Here are two examples:

> If your right eye causes you to sin, gouge it out and throw it away. It is better for you to lose one part of your body than for your whole body to be thrown into hell. And if your right hand causes you to sin, cut it off and throw it away. It is better for you to lose one part of your body than for your whole body to go into hell. (Mt 5:29-30 NIV)

> If anyone comes to me and does not hate his father and mother, his wife and children, his brothers and sisters—yes, even his own life—he cannot be my disciple. (Lk 14:26 NIV)

A literal reading of the first text might lead a person to engage in self-mutilation, but this would be to miss the real message Jesus is trying to convey. By exaggerating he is pointing out how ridiculous it is for anyone to allow the apparent joys of one sin to overshadow the very real horror of eternal damnation. By overstating his case, he accents in a striking way the necessity of setting sin aside.

Similarly, in first-century Palestine, where Jesus' audience would have been quite accustomed to hyperbolic claims, it is unlikely that the second example, cited from Luke's Gospel, would have been understood woodenly. Far from insisting that following Jesus means hating one's family, Jesus is asserting that no loyalty can stand in the way of one's allegiance to his lordship. In such cases as these, the reader's ability to discern Jesus' use of exaggeration is vital to proper understanding of Jesus' sayings.

Irony

A third device for effective communication in which language is used in a less-than-straightforward manner is irony. Here, we are concerned with "the subtle use of contrast between what is actually stated and what is more or less wryly suggested."[5] A helpful if rather lengthy example of Jesus' use of irony is found in the parable of the Good Samaritan (Lk 10:29-37). For Jesus'

audience the Samaritan would have represented those outside
the limits of God's grace, those incapable of neighborly response. In demonstrating compassion after the Jewish leaders
had failed to do so, the Samaritan exploded the hearers' preconceptions. In this story, then, the irony consists in the dramatic reversal of roles among the characters.

A further example can be found in the introduction to the
"seven woes" Jesus pronounces on the Pharisees and teachers
of the law: "The teachers of the law and the Pharisees sit in
Moses' seat. So you must obey them and do everything they tell
you" (Mt 23:2-3 NIV).

In this instance, we hear Jesus making a rather surprising
assertion, for he seems to be underscoring the legitimate, even
divine, authority of the Jewish leaders. Listening to the text as
it proceeds, however, we realize that Jesus is actually speaking
ironically, even sarcastically: The very ones who should lead
the people of God (as Moses did) are working toward their
destruction. As with hyperbolic statements, statements of irony
embrace a meaning which does not correspond strictly to the
words employed. They must be understood in the spirit in
which they were given.

There are numerous other devices Jesus used by way of communicating his message—proverbial sayings, questions, puns,
riddles and so on. We have discussed these three forms of
communication because of their significance in the *interpretive*
process. Due to the way they employ language to convey meaning, they present special problems to the reader who is not
attuned to the fact that Jesus did not always communicate in
straightforward prose.

Word in Deed

Before taking a closer look at another form of communication
Jesus used, the parable, we must recognize that there is much
more to Jesus' *message* than what he *said*. It is true that when
discussing the message of Jesus most people have focused on
his words—that is, his verbal communication. Thus, the important New Testament scholar Norman Perrin has written no less

than three books on Jesus' message, each of which focuses especially on teaching or language to recapture something of Jesus' importance. Even a conservative scholar like Gordon-Conwell's Royce Gordon Gruenler, whose book promises *New Approaches to Jesus and the Gospels,* appears to be fascinated almost exclusively with Jesus' words. Stein himself, in explicating *The Method and Message of Jesus' Teaching,* does little more than recognize the importance of Jesus' *actions* for an understanding of his message.[6]

At best, this approach to understanding Jesus and the Gospels is incomplete and unbalanced. At worst, it radically distorts the message of Jesus and the Gospels. After all, the evangelists were obviously concerned to tell something of what Jesus *did* as well as what he *said.* The Gospels are narratives, not collections of sayings. Moreover, like sayings told in unexpected ways or with surprising punch lines, extraordinary actions have the ability to place a permanent stamp on the minds of an audience.

Most important, as with any person, Jesus' actions provided the canon by which his teaching was measured. Or as we might say, Did he practice what he preached? Jesus' nonverbal communication, then, might be regarded as the embodiment of his message, the incarnation of the gospel. His deeds complement, affirm and legitimize his verbal communication.

The close relationship between the verbal and nonverbal message is evident in a narrative like Mark 2:1-12. This is the well-known story of the paralyzed man who was let down to Jesus through an opening in the roof. Jesus' *message* provides the climax of the narrative, and it is communicated in two seemingly distinct ways. Verbally, Jesus declares forgiveness of sins. Nonverbally, he heals the paralytic. As he himself makes clear, however, the two actions are the same (vv. 9-10).

What are some of Jesus' deeds which especially help us to understand who he was? Above all else stands Jesus' table fellowship with sinners. In chapter three we discussed the extraordinary character of this deed, and in doing so underscored its theological significance. In breaking bread with sinners, Jesus brought them God's salvation, demonstrating in real life (and not empty words) that God's redemptive purpose embraced all kinds of people—non-Jews and outcasts alike. It is difficult to imagine how Jesus would have gained the respect and following he did if his behavior had not in this way illustrated and embodied his verbal proclamation.

The Miracle Worker

The philosophical debate against miracles aside,[7] there can be no doubt that Jesus was known as a miracle worker. This is consistent with his portrait in the Gospels, and the Acts narrative remembers Jesus as "a man accredited by God . . . by miracles, wonders and signs" (2:22 NIV; see also 10:38). Jesus' activity as a miracle worker may even be at the root of the charges brought against him which led to his crucifixion. According to Deuteronomy 13:1-5, false prophets would appear, winning appeal through miraculous acts, but leading God's people astray. That Jesus might have been regarded as a false prophet of this kind is clear in the indictment brought against him: "We have found this man subverting our nation. . . . He stirs up the people all over Judea by his teaching" (Lk 23:2, 5 NIV).

The Gospels provide a portrait in which Jesus' miracles were integral to his self-understanding and ministry. This is certainly clear in the Third Gospel where, in a programmatic speech before a synagogue audience in Nazareth, he proclaims the fulfillment of prophecy in his coming (Lk 4:16-21). Quoting from Isaiah 61:1-2, Jesus claims for himself a ministry of proclamation and healing. Later, when asked by John the Baptist's disciples if he was the "Expected One," Jesus replies, "Go back and report to John what you have seen and heard: The blind receive sight, the lame walk, those who have leprosy are cured, the deaf hear, the dead are raised, and the good news is preached to the poor" (Lk 7:22 NIV). Interestingly, Luke thus reports that miraculous acts were integral to Jesus' understanding of his own ministry.

Given that the Gospels report Jesus as a miracle worker, what is the significance of his miraculous acts? Most generally *and* importantly, Jesus' miracles marked the coming of God's final, eschatological intervention in his ministry. Thus, after Jesus raised a widow's son, the people responded with awe, saying to one another, "God has come to save his people" (Lk 7:11-17). When Jesus healed a man who was blind and mute in Matthew's narrative, "all the people were astonished and said, 'Could this be the Son of David?' " (12:22-23 NIV). This narrated event gives rise to a discussion of the origin of Jesus' power, some claiming it derived from Beelzebub (the devil). Jesus insisted to the contrary that it was by the Spirit of God that he drove out demons, and that this itself was a demonstration that the kingdom of God has come (12:24-28). Through every act of overturning disease and death, Jesus demonstrated that the evil one was overcome. His miraculous acts proclaim a loud message: In his presence and work, the kingdom of God has come!

Jesus and Outcasts

In writing to the Christians of Galatia, Paul was able to affirm, "There is neither Jew nor Greek, slave nor free, male nor female, for you are all one in Christ Jesus" (Gal 3:28 NIV). In doing so, Paul was only affirming in writing what Jesus had already demonstrated in deed. In associating with Gentiles, Samaritans, "sinners," lepers and others, Jesus broke through the barriers which had been built up over years and years of Jewish life. In upholding a Gentile soldier as a model for faith (Lk 7:1-10), in counting women among his followers (Lk 8:1-3), and in calling a tax collector to discipleship (Mk 2:13-14), Jesus demonstrated that the good news of God's salvation knew no boundaries. Activity of this nature could only be regarded as scandalous in its day, but through such deeds Jesus embodied his gospel, proving its message was not empty.

Beyond these, there were other important deeds in Jesus' ministry—including the Last Supper, his selection of *twelve* core disciples, the footwashing episode, the cleansing of the temple, and so on. By mentioning three—table fellowship with sinners, miraculous acts and association with outcasts, we have empha-

sized the need to develop a sensitivity to the theological significance of Jesus' actions. After all, no person, least of all Jesus,
is all talk.

Conclusion

While the sayings of Jesus form an important means by which
the Gospels communicate their message, these sayings themselves employ various forms or devices. We have looked at
three, all of which use words and phrases in less direct ways to
convey the message. In doing so, we have accented the need
to read carefully, but imaginatively, allowing the words to paint
pictures in our minds and speak to us in less direct ways. We
have also seen that Jesus' message encompasses more than
words, however. His deeds constitute a "proclaimed word" in
their own right, possessing sometimes profound meaning in
terms of God's redemptive plan. Through word and deed, Jesus
communicates the gospel which he himself incarnates.

10
Parables
in Jesus'
Teaching

In his fourth chapter, Mark reports of Jesus that "he did not say anything to them without using a parable" (4:34 NIV). While in terms of Jesus' total ministry this statement would be an exaggeration, the parable is nevertheless the manner of teaching we most closely associate with Jesus' public teaching.

Parables like that of the Prodigal Son or of the Sower are widely known. Yet, of all the ways Jesus chose to communicate his message, none is more extraordinary to the modern reader than the parable, for in many ways the parable is alien to our way of thinking. To people reared on reading, writing and arithmetic—all primarily leading to a logical, prosaic, nonmetaphorical view of reality—the parable must seem a mysterious form of communication.[1] This fact is demonstrated best by observing the number of preachers and teachers who feel compelled to explain a parable's message in straightforward, propositional statements.

We are devoting a chapter to Jesus' use of parables because of their importance in his ministry and their strangeness to modern readers of the Gospels. We will first describe the general nature of parables and then move on to discuss several fac-

tors which determine how a parable can best be understood
today.

What Is a Parable?

Our word *parable* derives from the Greek term *parabolē* which
signifies "comparison." This sets us on our way to understanding the general nature of a parable. However, beyond this
broad description, we must also recognize that the evangelists
give the name *parable* to a variety of related phenomena.[2] That
is, parables appear in various guises.

First is the *similitude,* which is a developed simile (explicit
comparison). While a simple simile might explain something
(for example, the kingdom of God) in view of its likeness to
something else (say, a treasure), the similitude expands the
picture to explain the basis for comparison. Thus instead of
saying simply "the kingdom of heaven is like a treasure," Jesus
says, "The kingdom of heaven is like treasure hidden in a field.
When a man found it, he hid it again, and then in his joy went
out and sold all he had and bought that field" (Mt 13:44 NIV).
The similitude is amply illustrated further by the string of comparisons in Matthew 13:24-50.

Second is the *story parable*—inclusive of an introduction, conclusion, cast of characters and simple plot. The most familiar
example of this type of parable is probably the Good Samaritan
(Lk 10:30-35). Other examples of the story parable include the
Prodigal Son (Lk 15:11-32), the Two Debtors (Lk 7:41-43), the
Ten Virgins (Mt 25:1-13) and the Two Sons (Mt 21:28-31)—to
mention only a few.

Some parables—the story of the Wicked Tenants (Mk 12:1-9),
for example—are *allegorical* in character, though we should be
clear about how we are using this word. In employing the term
allegory I am not suggesting that every detail in this or other
parables must be regarded as significant. Nor am I arguing that
the key for unlocking the meaning of a parable should be
found outside the parable itself. Thus I am not suggesting that
we follow the example of Augustine, that otherwise important
figure in the early history of the church. He provides us with

a classic example of the allegorical interpretation of parables gone awry in his treatment of the story of the Good Samaritan:

> *A certain man went down from Jerusalem to Jericho;* Adam himself is meant; *Jerusalem* is the heavenly city of peace, from whose blessedness Adam fell; *Jericho* means the moon, and signifies our mortality, because it is born, waxes, wanes, and dies. *Thieves* are the devil and his angels.[3]

And so on. In this way, Augustine uses his understanding of redemptive history as the "code" for unlocking the meaning of the parable. This is not the kind of *allegorical interpretation* I have in mind when I credit some parables with allegorical elements.[4]

Nevertheless some details in parables provide more than "color" and "background" for the central point of the story. They are themselves central to the parable, helping to determine the meaning of the story. In some cases, the hearers are intended to identify the details and characters of the story with real historical referents. In the parable of the Wicked Tenants, for example, there can be little doubt about the historical referents of certain details.

Jesus himself intends as much for, in telling his story, he has chosen to build on an allegory already familiar to his audience due to its presence in Isaiah 5:1-7. In this Old Testament text the vineyard is "the house of Israel, the men of Judah," the possession of "the LORD Almighty." Allegorical elements, then, are built into Jesus' parable. Indeed Mark records that the Jewish leaders were not slow to understand the point of the story: *They* were the tenants who would be destroyed for their wickedness (Mk 12:12).

Recognition of elements such as this in parables raises important questions for modern readers. What does the parable form try to do? What is its purpose? And how does it achieve that purpose?

The Function of Parable

It is now generally understood that parables are not primarily designed to teach a lesson but to bring about a response. Even

those parables which seem bent on defining the kingdom of
God (for example, see Mk 4:26-32) are not pedagogy pure and
simple. They, too, intend to confront the listener with the necessity of a present and radical decision for the kingdom.

Parables then are not meant to pat us on the back but to give
us a kick in the pants. They are not intended to comfort us but
to challenge us and change us. Parables speak out against the
status quo; they call into question the way we understand the
world and God's activity in it; they sweep away our preconceptions. As John Dominic Crossan has put it, "Parable is always
a somewhat unnerving experience. You can usually recognize
a parable because your immediate reaction will be self-contra-
dictory: 'I don't know what you mean by that story but I'm
certain I don't like it.' "[5] Parables are the demonstrators waving
signs of protest, speaking out against our ways of thinking, our
traditional ways of experiencing and obeying God, our spiritual
institutions.

What Is the Point?
How do parables achieve this end? Almost a whole generation
of scholars has argued that parables function by emphasizing
one point and one point only. Thus, in their more popular
treatment of biblical interpretation, Fee and Stuart subtitle their
chapter on parables with the question "Do you get the
point?"—as if to say that a parable has only one point which
must be grasped if we are to understand at all what the parable
is saying.[6] No doubt, this emphasis is a reaction to the allego-
rizing tendencies in parable interpretation we have noted
above. Unfortunately, like the excessive allegorization of parables, this more modern emphasis is excessive in its own way.

Consider, for example, the parable of the Sower (Mk 4:3-8
and parallels). Several main points are at work here. (1) Grace
is evident in the sower's indiscriminate sowing on both good
and bad soil. (2) Judgment and obstacles to growth are present
in that not every seed produces fruit. (3) On the other hand,
hope is present for, we are assured, some seed does bear fruit.
(4) Producing fruit is an essential characteristic of the kingdom.

(5) The use of seeds and the closely associated ideas of growth and elapsed time point out that the kingdom comes not instantaneously but over time.

All of these ideas are present, and all are important lessons regarding the nature of the kingdom. To be sure, they are not unrelated and together they serve a larger goal—namely, to underscore the necessity of hearing the word and producing fruit. But to name this as the overarching call of the parable is not the same thing as suggesting that it intends only one idea.

In his study of the parables, Kenneth Bailey suggests a helpful model for understanding how parables work to call the listener/reader to respond.[7] He notes that a parable may use a variety of images which correspond to things familiar to the listener. The world of ideas presented by the parable thus stands in tension with the listener's world of ideas. At the intersection of the two the listener is called to respond. The following diagram, adapted from Bailey's, illustrates this model:

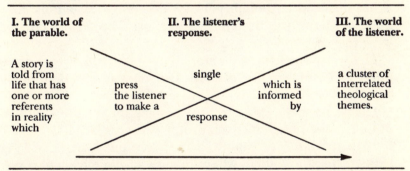

I. The world of the parable.	II. The listener's response.	III. The world of the listener.
A story is told from life that has one or more referents in reality which	press the listener to make a __single__ __response__	which is informed by	a cluster of interrelated theological themes.

Thus, the listener is pressed by the many themes of the parable of the Sower to make a single response—to receive the message of the kingdom and, having done so, to produce fruit befitting the kingdom.

The point of a parable, then, is to call the listener to respond. In doing so, the parable draws on things that are familiar to the listener. By means of comparison, it communicates a challenging theological message. A parable told for one group of people, then, might mean little or nothing to another group which does not share its world of ideas. There are at least two ways of getting around this problem—coming to terms with the background and interpretation of the ancient story and retelling it in modern terms. The two are closely related, as we shall see in what follows.

The Cultural Problem

A key problem facing readers of Jesus' parables today is that his stories were intended for a first-century Palestinian audience, and we are not that audience. They thus presume a realm of ideas and debate with which we are not necessarily familiar. Sometimes this obstacle is not completely insurmountable, and we may understand something of the message even if we do not fully grasp its potential impact.

For example, an important aspect of the message of the parable of the Great Banquet (Lk 14:16-24) is clear to us even if we fail to understand all of the particulars of the plot. Without much effort we might realize that Jesus is saying something about those who, though perhaps deserving invitations, turn them down, only to be replaced by those who do not deserve to be invited.

The story may have even more impact for us, however, if we understand some of the following dynamics at work behind the parable:

1. The banquet was a common metaphor for the kingdom of God, as we noted in chapter three (see also Lk 14:15).

2. In that ancient culture, a host sent out invitations long before a feast and then, when the time of the feast had come, sent out his messengers only to those who accepted the invitation. That is, the people who now refuse to dine in this parable are those who had already received *and* accepted a prior invitation.

3. An invitation to a banquet was a sign of social status. Unlike such matters today (where we might receive more invitations than we have nights), such an invitation was too great an honor to lightly refuse.

4. The excuses given, in every case, were ridiculously lame and are cast in forms which provide the greatest possible hu-

miliation to the banquet host.

5. Among some of Jesus' contemporaries it was thought that "defective Jews" (that is, those "of the town" who were poor, crippled, etc. [vs. 21]) would have no place at the great feast of the kingdom of God.

6. Similarly, Gentiles (that is, those from "the roads and country lanes" [vs. 23]) were excluded from the kingdom in much Jewish speculation.

7. In the Judaism of Jesus' day, the idea of a "full number" was associated with speculation about who would be granted a place in the kingdom (see Lk 13:23). Hence, in this parable, those who first received invitations (and those hearing the parable) would be astounded that the banquet hall could be filled to capacity (vs. 23) by Jewish outcasts and Gentiles.

All of these factors and more highlight the profoundly radical character of the message embodied in this parable.

Of course, the message of the parable of the Great Banquet is not completely out of our reach, but this story does demonstrate a basic difficulty we have in reading the parables today. Jesus' parables presume a culture which is twenty centuries removed from our own. They draw their pointedness from a setting which is, more or less, alien to us. Thus, for example, we will never really be struck by the message of the Good Samaritan until we purge our minds of any notion that a *Samaritan* could possibly be *"good"*![8]

What I am emphasizing, then, is the need for us to be engaged in good historical study into the realm of ideas represented in the parables. For such study, there is no better place to begin than with serious reflection on the world represented by the Gospels themselves. As first-century documents, they obviously represent something of the world of ideas of their time. Beyond this, commentaries and Bible dictionaries can be of help, but do not overlook the number of fresh and helpful studies being conducted today on the sociology of the ancient world.[9] Despite the relative paucity of firm data, these studies open up for us in new ways the culture of everyday men and women in the ancient world.

Parable and Gospel

One further clue as to how a parable may be understood is its *function* in its literary context. How does the shape of the narrative as a whole help determine the sense of a parable? How does the evangelist make use of the parable in his larger story? In other words, when reading a parable we are interested in more than the message of the parable viewed as an isolated literary unit. Indeed, when reading the Gospels as larger, self-contained stories, we are far more interested in how the parable sheds light on the larger narrative, and how the larger narrative sheds light on the parable. Our question then becomes, How does the *evangelist* make use of this story?

Take, for example, the parable of the Wicked Tenants (Mk 12:1-9). In the section just preceding the parable in Mark (that is, in Mk 11:27-33), the issue at stake is the source of Jesus' authority. At the end of this debate, Jesus explicitly refuses to tell the Jewish leaders "by what authority I am doing these things." Yet, in positioning the parable of the Wicked Tenants after this story, Mark's Gospel *by means of the parable* answers the question raised by the Jewish leaders. Jesus is the son who was loved by the owner of the vineyard, the heir who would be killed by the wicked tenants. His source of authority, then, is his father, the Lord God himself.

Again, in Luke 14, one sees this principle at work. Here we find Jesus dining at the home of a Pharisee, where Jesus reportedly dialogs with the dinner guests about places of honor and banquet invitations. The parable of the Great Banquet is introduced by a rather abrupt observation on the part of an anonymous dinner guest regarding those who will eat at the kingdom feast. In this context, then, the parable of the Great Banquet highlights and illustrates Jesus' earlier, nonparabolic instruction. Moreover, it calls those whom Jesus invites to "my banquet" to accept the invitation (14:24).

The Parable and the Modern Reader

Our earlier comments about the relation of the parable to its own context (historical and literary) have been leading us to an important question: How can the parables of Jesus best speak to us? The first answer has been given. We can give ourselves to understanding the cultural phenomena behind the text and thus, in a sense, be transformed into first-century men and women. There is some validity to this approach, for it allows Jesus' message to encounter us in a challenging way that calls for our response to the kingdom. Similarly, we can inquire into the literary context of the parable and see how a certain story communicated as a part of the Gospel framework.

However, in the end, this backward-looking method is inadequate, for we are not really first-century men and women. In the end, we must frame Jesus' message in images suitable to our own time and place. What images we employ will depend on the shape and color of our own culture. Nevertheless, one thing is clear: The message we communicate must strike the same nerves and call for the same response as the original parable did. We are not implying, therefore, that we need not do our homework in coming to terms with how Jesus' parables communicated in their first-century milieu. We are insisting, rather, that careful study of this kind is only the first step along the way to communicating that same message for our own culture.

An enlightening example of this expanded approach is offered by a look at the parable of the Good Samaritan (Lk 10:30-37). If we have done our homework on cultural background adequately, we will realize that this story is not a pleasant tale about caring for our next-door neighbor. Instead, it is a demand that we redefine *neighbor* to include "whoever is in need." In order to do so, we are told, we must put aside all prejudices—whether inherited or acquired; whether supported by observable evidence or not; whether religious, racial or social.

As abhorrent as the Samaritans were to the Jews (for whom *Samaritan* was a dirty word), there are, no doubt, people who are the object of equal hate and prejudice in our own circles. These are the very people we must now view as neighbors. For some, then, the tale of the Good Samaritan could be retold as the tale of the Good Nigger. If this seems a harsh contradiction in terms—a positive adjective related to a slang word with strongly negative connotations—this is only proof that we have struck the same chord as Jesus' parable would have in its historical setting.

For others the tale could be recast as the Good Feminist, the Good Russian, the Good Homosexual, the Good Millionaire, the Good Socialist, the Good Street Person, the Good Warmonger, the Good Sexist, the Good Wetback, the Good Roman Catholic, the Good Capitalist or the Good Addict. No less than the first-century Jew, modern men and women have their own ways of drawing lines and excluding others. In order to be faithful to Jesus' message, we must learn the parable of the Good Samaritan for our own circumstances—and hear its radical demand that love be extended to all.

The Fallacy of Interpretation

No doubt, all of the points we have looked at regarding the interpretation of parables are vital to a proper reading of the Gospels. Nevertheless, there is a point at which the parable must no longer be regarded as an object for scrutiny and objective analysis.

> The refrain of Jesus with which [the parables] are laced, "Whoever has ears to hear, let him hear," invites the scholar to put aside his or her lexicons and concordances, to stop taking notes and just listen. . . . Very soon the scholar who "lets go" in this way will turn out to be no different in human reactions from a small child hearing Jesus' stories for the first time, or a bemused stranger to Christian faith pausing to listen to something oddly familiar, yet at the same time new and unsettling.[10]

It is true. We are better able to hear after having done our homework, but in the end we must sit back and simply listen. *Then* we are confronted by a message which speaks to us in surprising ways, which lays a divine claim on our lives, and which calls forth from us revolutionary responses.

They that have ears to hear, let them hear!

11
Jesus and the Kingdom of God

Woven into the fabric of the Gospels is one motif which dominates all others. This theme is the kingdom of God, and it sets the borders and provides the pattern for the message of the Gospels. To fail to understand the concept of the kingdom of God and its importance is to fail to understand the warp and woof of the Gospels.

The centrality of the kingdom to the Gospels is only a reflection of its dominance in the sayings and acts of Jesus. We do not exaggerate in declaring that the idea of the kingdom of God is the hub around which Jesus' ministry revolves.

Kingdom of God . . . or Heaven?

Of course, when referring to the "kingdom of God," we also intend to embrace the synonymous phrase "kingdom of heaven." The latter appears in the Gospels only in Matthew.[1] Why would one speak of the kingdom of heaven rather than that of God? In the Judaism of Jesus' day (and before), it was not unusual to substitute the name *God* with other names and descriptions. This practice resulted from the increasing tendency in Judaism to avoid using the divine name so as to ensure that the second commandment ("You shall not misuse the name of the LORD your God" [Ex 20:7 NIV; see also Deut 5:11]) was scrupulously observed.[2]

In the Gospels themselves are other examples of the use of circumlocutions of this kind for *God*—as in Mark 14:61-62. There, in the trial scene, Jesus is asked if he is the Son of the "Blessed One," and he replies that the Son of Man will be seen sitting at the right hand of the "Mighty One." Both expressions are substitutions or circumlocutions for God. In a Gospel like Matthew which is otherwise noted for its Jewish character the expression "kingdom of heaven," then, is not unexpected.

A further indication that "kingdom of God" and "kingdom of heaven" are only alternative expressions for the same reality is their use in synonymous statements. For example:

Matthew 13:11: He replied, "The knowledge of the secrets of the *kingdom of heaven* has been given to you." (NIV)

Mark 4:11: He told them, "The secret of the *kingdom of God* has been given to you." (NIV)

Luke 8:10: He said, "The knowledge of the secrets of the *kingdom of God* has been given to you." (NIV)

In these parallel texts, both Mark and Luke use the expression "kingdom of God" while Matthew has "kingdom of heaven." We conclude, for these reasons, that both phrases point to the same reality.

The Centrality of the Kingdom

The extraordinary significance of the kingdom for Jesus is underscored first by the frequency of the expression in his teaching. A simple count in the Synoptic Gospels reveals some eighty-five occurrences of "kingdom of God" or its equivalent "kingdom of heaven."

While "kingdom of God" occurs only twice in the Fourth Gospel, this should not be taken to indicate that the concept was unimportant. Quite the contrary, John underscores the significance of the kingdom as much as do the other evangelists, but in his own language. For an audience oriented more to Hellenism, "kingdom of God" would have little meaning.

Hence, John uses a substitute expression—"life" or "eternal life"—to communicate much the same idea.

In this John was not a radical innovator, however, for some Synoptic texts demonstrate that the identification between the kingdom and life had already been made. Mark 9:43, 45 and 47 provide a helpful illustration of this fact, for there the parallel expressions "enter life" and "enter the kingdom of God" are synonymous. All four Gospels are in agreement, therefore, on the frequency with which the idea of the kingdom of God is associated with Jesus' mission.

Even more significant than statistical evidence, however, are the summaries of Jesus' message recorded in the Gospels. For example, in Mark's Gospel we read: "After John was put in prison, Jesus went into Galilee, proclaiming the good news of God. 'The time has come,' he said. 'The kingdom of God has drawn near. Repent and believe the good news!' " (1:14-15).

Important parallels to this summary of Jesus' message occur in Matthew 4:17, 23; 9:35; Luke 4:43; 9:11; and Acts 1:3. This text in Mark does not intend to simply relate for us an isolated saying of Jesus, but instead to characterize the heart of Jesus' message. In fact, George Beasley-Murray has argued that Mark drew this passage from early catechetical teaching, where it provided the answer to the question, What was the message of Jesus?[3]

Precisely what this text means in terms of Jesus' understanding of the kingdom will be discussed below. For now, it is important that we note two things. First, the summary statement leaves no doubt as to the importance of the kingdom for Jesus. As such it provides weighty testimony to the centrality of the kingdom for Jesus' mission. This point is highlighted all the more by the parallel in Luke 4:43, where Jesus asserts that *the reason he was sent* was to "preach the good news of the kingdom of God."

Second, the terms of the summary in Mark 1:14-15 assume the familiarity of Jesus' audience with the expectation of the kingdom of God. Since Jesus provides no dictionary definition of "kingdom of God," we must assume that he was working with a concept already available to him in his religious environment. This assumption raises two or three questions. What was the prevailing expectation of the kingdom in Jesus' day? How were the people of Palestine prepared for Jesus' kingdom emphasis? How did he adopt or adapt their understanding of the kingdom?

The Long-Awaited Kingdom

Interestingly enough, the expression "kingdom of God" is absent from the Old Testament. Nevertheless, the idea of God's sovereign rule (the reality to which the kingdom language points) is very much present! This motif, God's rule, probably comes to clearest expression in the so-called enthronement psalms which explicitly proclaim, "Yahweh is King!" (for example, Ps 47, 93, and 96—99). Psalm 2 also reflects the idea of God's kingdom. In this psalm, Israel appears ultimately as a theocracy—with the Lord as the "Enthroned One" (v. 4) represented on earth by his "son" (vv. 6-7).

As Old Testament faith turned more and more to a forward-looking hope, orienting its faith toward the future, the people of God focused on the future realization of God's authority, rule and justice.[4] In order to lessen the tensions between their faith in a sovereign Lord and their experience of oppression, they began to restructure their theology.

As a result, God's people longed for and anticipated the coming of God's rule in future history, when the wicked (that is, "our enemies") would be judged and the righteous (that is, "we, the children of Israel") would experience the kingship of the Lord. Thus, for example, Isaiah 2:4 anticipates the justice, communion and peace to come, and Psalm 98:7-9 looks forward to the joy of all creation—when God will reign.

In intertestamental times, the anticipation of God's reign was extended along similar lines to that which had already been expressed in the Old Testament. According to that major stream of Judaism influenced by apocalyptic eschatology, the kingdom was a future reality to be instituted by God himself. The Lord, they believed, would intervene in a climactic, catastrophic way at the end of history. By way of illustration of this development, we may cite a first-century apocalyptic text:

And when the whole of creation, visible and invisible, which the LORD has created, shall come to an end, then each person will go to the LORD's great judgment. And then all time will perish, and afterward there will be neither years nor months nor days nor hours. They will be dissipated, and after that they will be not be reckoned.

But they will constitute a single age. And all the righteous, who escape from the LORD's great judgment, will be collected together into the great age. And the great age will come about for the righteous, and it will be eternal.

And after that there will be among them neither weariness nor sickness nor affliction nor worry nor want nor debilitation nor night nor darkness.

But they will have a great light, a great indestructible light, and paradise, great and incorruptible. For everything corruptible will pass away, and the incorruptible will come into being, and will be the shelter of the eternal residences. (2 Enoch 65:6-10)[5]

This represents an advance beyond the eschatological view of the Old Testament prophets. No longer is the kingdom understood in this-worldly terms (nationalistic, flesh-and-blood, etc.). The kingdom now appears in transcendent dress—emphasizing cosmic, universal and eternal dimensions.

Of course, this was not the only way of viewing things in the period just before and during the ministry of Jesus. The Zealots, for example, sought to cooperate with God in bringing the kingdom. Their perspective led them to employ even violent means to free themselves and all Israel from "worldly" (that is, alien) rule. To obey God was, for them, to refuse obedience to the Roman authorities.

Another Jewish sect, however, took a quite different approach. The people of Qumran actively separated themselves from mainstream Judaism and yet continued to expect that God's reign would one day be established. On the other hand, the people at Qumran apparently shared with the Zealots something of the view of the relation between the kingdom and warfare. They were prepared to engage in active struggle at the end, in the final, apocalyptic battle against the kingdom of darkness.

How can we summarize the idea of the kingdom prominent in the time of Jesus? Jesus' contemporaries believed that Yahweh was King, and that the time was coming when he would establish his sovereign reign over the whole world. It is this expectation Jesus spoke to when he proclaimed, "The time has come! The kingdom of God has drawn near!" How, then, did Jesus' understanding of the kingdom compare with that of his contemporaries?

Jesus and the Kingdom

The most pressing question regarding Jesus' understanding of the kingdom in light of pre-Christian thought concerns the meaning of the phrase the "kingdom of God *has drawn near*" (Mk 1:14-15).[6] With this assertion we are at the heart of the "debate of this century" regarding the nature of the kingdom in Jesus' teaching.[7] Was the kingdom an entity Jesus expected in the near future? Or had the kingdom already arrived?

A solution to this problem rests not so much on the Greek verb employed here (*engiken,* translated "has drawn near"), but on the relation of the two clauses in the summary statement. In fact, the two should be read in parallel, as pointing to the same reality:

"The time has come!"

"The kingdom of God has drawn near!"

Thus, Jesus is relating his ministry to the past expectation of the long-awaited kingdom (now fulfilled), but also pointing to the future coming of the kingdom. In Beasley-Murray's words, "the long awaited *time has now come* and the kingdom of God which is to embrace the whole world *has begun its course.*"[8]

This, then, is the point at which Jesus' proclamation of the kingdom departs from the expectations of his contemporaries. Unlike them (and unlike John the Baptist), he no longer merely anticipated the kingdom; he proclaimed its arrival in his ministry. The long-awaited time had come! If what Jesus proclaimed did not "look" like the kingdom, this was due to his understanding of how the kingdom would come about: It was both present and on the way to fulfillment.

Thus in describing the nature of the kingdom Jesus proclaimed, we need not choose between a *present* kingdom or a *future* one. Both time designations are embraced. This is clear not only from Mark 1:14-15, but also from the tension between present and future in Jesus' ministry. That the kingdom of God is to be manifested in the *future* is a repeated emphasis in Jesus' teaching. It lies at the heart of the "Lord's Prayer"—explicitly in the phrase Jesus taught his followers to pray, "Your kingdom come!" and implicitly in the whole (Mt 6:9-13; Lk 11:2-4). Many of Jesus' parables define the kingdom in eschatological images awaiting fulfillment. The Wedding Banquet (Mt 22:1-14), the Weeds (Mt 13:24-30) and the Ten Virgins (Mt 25:1-13) are only three pertinent examples. Again and again in Mark 13 the disciples are told, Watch! for the time of the end will come, though we know not when.

On the other hand, the *presence* of the kingdom is presumed and declared throughout Jesus' ministry. As we have seen in earlier chapters, Jesus proclaimed the presence of the kingdom in his actions, particularly in his table fellowship with sinners and his miraculous deeds. Hence, he openly declares that his ministry of exorcism is a sign that the kingdom of God "has come upon you" (Mt 11:28; see also Mk 3:27). As Schillebeeckx has observed,

> The gospels make it clear that a salvation which does not manifest itself here and now, in respect to concrete, individual human beings, can have nothing in the way of "glad tidings" about it. The dawning of God's rule becomes visible on this earth, within our history, through every victory over the "powers of evil." This it is that the miracles of Jesus exemplify.[9]

Jesus' activity—which expresses the inclusive love and power of God—reveals the presence of God's rule. His sayings, too, proclaim the presence of the kingdom through his ministry (see, for example, Lk 17:20-21). Why, then, was the kingdom not more apparent? The parables of growth anticipate and defuse doubts of this nature. The present kingdom is not shown such that all can recognize its presence. Rather, it is like a seed growing, though we do not understand how (Mk 4:26-29). It is like a mustard seed—an insignificant thing, it would seem— and yet a thing which achieves unsurpassed glory (Mk 4:30-32).

We have thus looked at three major developments in kingdom expectation. The first was the prophetic, which visualized God's intervention *in* history, a divine act which would mark the beginning of life in God's kingdom *in* history. The second was the apocalyptic, which visualized God's intervention *at the end of* history, a divine act which would mark the beginning of life in God's kingdom *beyond* history. The third was the understanding of Jesus, who proclaimed that God had intervened in history in Jesus' own person and mission, thus initiating the time of the kingdom. The time of the kingdom therefore overlaps with present history, at the end of which Jesus will return and the kingdom will be consummated.

Given the present-not-yet character of the kingdom, it is certainly worth asking, Where is the kingdom? Or what sort of kingdom is this? In earlier centuries, Christians were willing to identify the kingdom with the church, for they saw the church as the focal point of God's sovereign rule.[10] More recently Christians have been reluctant to continue this identification, pointing to the provisional and sinful character of the church.[11] Behind this discussion is a more fundamental issue—namely, how the term *kingdom* ought to be understood. Should it be defined in terms of the physical realm in which God's reign is exercised (that is, concretely) or as that reign itself (that is, abstractly)? Generally speaking, modern scholars have been keen to favor the idea of God's *reign* over that of a *realm*. Here again, though, we must ask whether we are not being offered a false dichotomy.

At the most basic level, we can never ignore the importance of the land for Israel's faith. The land is where God's redemptive activity takes place. Of course, in certain strands of the developing eschatology of the Old Testament—especially that in Isaiah and Daniel, the idea of the land was universalized to embrace the whole world. This motif should warn us against choosing a purely abstract view of the kingdom over against a more concrete, physical perception.

From a different approach, Howard Marshall has noted that "the [kingdom of God] is not just the sovereign rule of God; it is also the set-up created by the activity of God, and that set-up consists of people."[12] For Marshall, this "set-up" is "the church as the people of God." While we might want to define this "set-up" more broadly than he has done, in order to embrace the cosmic dimensions of God's inbreaking kingdom, his view nevertheless succeeds in pushing us past either-or distinctions on this issue. The kingdom, then, is *God's reign as it comes to expression in God's world and as it is realized in and through God's people.*

The Son of Man and the Kingdom

What is it that holds these tensions together in the teaching of Jesus in the Gospels? It is Jesus' teaching regarding the Son of Man. But who is this Son of Man with whom Jesus identifies himself?[13] In the vernacular of Jesus' day, the sense of "Son of Man" in some contexts could have been tantamount to saying "I." On the other hand, building on the foundational passage in Daniel 7:13-14, "Son of Man" could be a heavenly figure, the "Son of Man" understood as a title of divinity.[14] In the Danielic sense, the Son of Man represents above all else the people of God. He gains an everlasting kingdom, and through him it is manifest in the world. Jesus, then, employed an ambiguous phrase as a self-designation, and so expressed his self-understanding in a veiled way.

As the Son of Man, Jesus would have seen his role as that of creating and gathering together the people of God into the eternal kingdom. This he has done by means of his earthly ministry as the Son of Man (see, for example, Mk 2:10; Lk 19:10) and his death and resurrection (see especially Mk 8:31; 9:31; 10:45). When Jesus returns as the Son of Man in glory (see, for example, Mk 8:38; 13:24-27; 14:62; Mt 25:31-46), he will bring his work to completion. His coming again will mark the end of history and the beginning of life in the fullness of the kingdom. Thus, the Son of Man sayings embrace Jesus' ministry, death, resurrection and coming again. In this way they demonstrate the essential unity of the present and future kingdom. Life in the kingdom, present and future, is inseparably related to the one mission of the Son of Man.

What is it that holds together the tensions essential to Jesus' understanding of the kingdom? Jesus himself, for the kingdom is present and will be brought to completion through his activity as the Son of Man.[15]

The message of the kingdom is therefore really a message about Jesus—the significance of his ministry, his death, his resurrection and his return. And this message is the heartbeat of the Gospels.

Epilogue

First-century Palestine, the time and place of Jesus and the Gospels, seems so far away at times. In a day when even the ancient art of working with wood is subject to the latest in design and laser technologies, the world of Jesus may appear strange and removed, primitive somehow. These differences, when taken seriously, throw up obstacles for readers of the Gospels. These obstacles are not insurmountable, but they are nonetheless real. The preceding chapters were designed to help identify and overcome those obstacles, to somehow bridge the chasms of time and space separating us from the Gospel stories.

Coming to terms with the historical realities of Jesus and the Gospels is not for Christians a mere exercise in dispelling curiosity, however. No matter how long ago those stories took place, their ability to speak a profound truth to us has not diminished. While we may know little of camels passing through the eyes of needles, and perhaps even less of the etiquette of washing feet and anointing heads, we may nevertheless encounter Jesus, our Risen Lord, in the pages of the Gospels of Matthew, Mark, Luke and John. We want to understand as much as we can about what the Gospel writers were doing, and why they were doing it. But in the end we are called to hear their message, to listen to God speaking to us through these writings, and to respond accordingly.

The Gospels spoke an authoritative and needed word from God in their own day. For those with ears to hear, they still do.

Notes

Chapter 1: An Introduction to Reading the Gospels
[1]See, for example, Acts 2:36; Rom 10:9; 1 Cor 12:3.
[2]See Eduard Schweizer, *Luke: A Challenge to Present Theology* (Atlanta: John Knox, 1982), pp. 41-55.

Chapter 2: One Gospel—Four Gospels
[1]This will be discussed further in part two.
[2]See James M. Robinson, ed., *The Nag Hammadi Library in English* (San Francisco: Harper & Row, 1977); Edgar Hennecke, *New Testament Apocrypha*, 2 vols., ed. Wilhelm Schneemelcher (Philadelphia: Westminster, 1963-65).
[3]Brevard S. Childs, *The New Testament as Canon: An Introduction* (London: SCM, 1984).
[4]See I. Howard Marshall, *Biblical Inspiration* (Grand Rapids, Mich.: Eerdmans, 1982).
[5]See chapter eleven.
[6]So, for example, John Howard Yoder, *The Politics of Jesus* (Grand Rapids, Mich.: Eerdmans, 1972); Nicholas Wolterstorff, *Until Justice and Peace Embrace* (Grand Rapids, Mich.: Eerdmans, 1983).
[7]This example was inspired by conversations with Dr. David Milikan.
[8]Gordon D. Fee and Douglas Stuart, *How to Read the Bible for All Its Worth: A Guide to Understanding the Bible* (Grand Rapids, Mich.: Zondervan, 1981), p. 111.
[9]The most recent defense of this viewpoint is Christopher M. Tuckett, *The Revival of the Griesbach Hypothesis: An Analysis and Appraisal* (Cambridge: Cambridge University, 1983). One alternative which has gained a number

of supporters is that Matthew was written first, was used as a source by Luke, and that Mark made use of both Matthew and Luke—see the now-classic discussion in William R. Farmer, *The Synoptic Problem* (Macon, Ga: Mercer University, 1976). A summary of Farmer's arguments is found in his *Jesus and the Gospel: Tradition, Scripture, and Canon* (Philadelphia: Fortress, 1982), pp. 1-11.

[10]For this discussion, see, for example, Leon Morris, "The Relationship of the Fourth Gospel to the Synoptics," in *Studies in the Fourth Gospel* (Exeter: Paternoster, 1969), pp. 15-63. For the alternative view, see C. K. Barrett, *The Gospel according to St. John*, 2d ed. (Philadelphia: Westminster, 1978), pp. 42-54. I have defended both conclusions stated in the text—namely, the priority of Mark and the independence of John—in my "The Death of Jesus: Tradition and Interpretation in the Passion Narrative" (Ph.D. diss., University of Aberdeen, 1985; forthcoming from J. C. B. Mohr [Paul Siebeck], Tübingen), pp. 43-59, 245-84.

Chapter 3: Jesus in Historical Context

[1]Geza Vermes is certainly right to make the point that Christians would do well to take more seriously Jesus' Jewishness—even if he fails to recognize how Christians view the significance of Jesus' resurrection and his uniqueness over against Judaism (*Jesus the Jew: A Historian's Reading of the Gospels* [Philadelphia: Fortress, 1973]; *Jesus and the World of Judaism* [London: SCM, 1983]). A recent and far-reaching study of the historical Jesus is *Jesus and the Constraints of History*, by A. E. Harvey (Philadelphia: Westminster, 1982). Harvey capitalizes on the observation that in order for Jesus and his message to be comprehensible to the people of his day, he had to work to a large degree within the constraints imposed on him by his culture.

[2]See Kenneth E. Bailey, *Poet & Peasant and Through Peasant Eyes: A Literary-Cultural Approach to the Parables in Luke,* combined ed. (Grand Rapids, Mich.: Eerdmans, 1983).

[3]Introductions to this period are now legion. For a good overview, see Robert A. Spivey and D. Moody Smith, *Anatomy of the New Testament: A Guide to Its Structure and Meaning,* 3d ed. (New York: Macmillan, 1982), pp. 9-56. Of continuing value are F. F. Bruce, *New Testament History* (Garden City, N.Y.: Doubleday, 1969), pp. 1-162; Eduard Lohse, *The New Testament Environment* (Nashville: Abingdon, 1976).

[4]Unfortunately for most American readers, the major works on Jesus' table fellowship with sinners have appeared at the hand of German scholars. For a brief but insightful treatment of the subject in English, see Ben F. Meyer, *The Aims of Jesus* (London: SCM, 1979), pp. 158-62.

[5]In Mark 2:17 we read "I came (ἦλθον) not to call the righteous, but sinners." A similar formula appears in Mark 10:45, and we should note that Jesus thus makes use of his own "technical term" for describing his mission.

[6]John Bright, *The History of Israel*, 2d ed. (Philadelphia: Westminster, 1972), p. 348.

[7]See especially, Christopher Rowland, *Christian Origins: An Account of the Setting and Character of the Most Important Messianic Sect of Judaism* (London: SPCK, 1985), part two.

[8]See E. P. Sanders, *Paul and Palestinian Judaism: A Comparison of Patterns of Religion* (London: SCM, 1977), especially part one; Rowland, *Christian Origins*, pp. 25-28.

[9]On the importance of Exodus-language in biblical thought, see G. B. Caird, *The Language and Imagery of the Bible* (London: Duckworth, 1980), p. 156. On the theme of the covenant, see William Dyrness, *Themes in Old Testament Theology* (Downers Grove, Ill.: InterVarsity), pp. 113-26; Gerhard F. Hasel, *Covenant in Blood* (Mountain View, Calif.: Pacific, 1982); Walther Eichrodt, *Theology of the Old Testament*, 2 vols. (Philadelphia: Fortress, 1961-67).

[10]Rowland, *Christian Origins*, p. 29. See also Dyrness, *Themes in Old Testament Theology*, chapters 1-3, 6.

[11]This text from Deuteronomy has been widely accepted as a creedal statement—see above all, Gerhard von Rad, *The Problem of the Hexateuch and Other Essays* (New York: McGraw-Hill, 1966), pp. 1-78; *Old Testament Theology*, 2 vols. (New York: Harper & Row, 1962-65) 1:121-23. Contra Peter C. Craigie, *The Book of Deuteronomy* (Grand Rapids, Mich.: Eerdmans, 1976), p. 321.

[12]For a survey of this material, see E. P. Sanders, *Jesus and Judaism* (London: SCM, 1985), pp. 77-90.

[13]The classic study on this period is Martin Hengel, *Judaism and Hellenism: Studies in Their Encounter in Palestine during the Early Hellenistic Period*, 2 vols. in 1 (Philadelphia: Fortress, 1974).

[14]Of course, this was not the only change in the theology of death during this era. In particular, this period saw the rise of a more explicit hope of resurrection and the understanding of the "effectiveness" of the death of martyrs—as an act atoning for one's own sins or even the sins of the nation. See, for example, 1 Macc 2:29-41; 2 Macc 6:18-8:5; Walter Brueggemann, "Death, Theology of," in *Interpreter's Dictionary of the Bible*, Supplementary Volume (Nashville: Abingdon, 1976), pp. 219-21; von Rad, *OT Theology*, 1:387-91; D. S. Russell, *The Method and Message of Jewish Apocalyptic* (London: SCM, 1964), pp. 353-57.

[15]Emil Schürer, *The History of the Jewish People in the Age of Jesus Christ (175 B.C.—A.D. 135)*, vol. 2, rev. ed., ed. Geza Vermes, Fergus Millar and Matthew Black (Edinburgh: T. & T. Clark, 1979), pp. 454-55.

[16]For the story of the Jewish revolt against Rome, see the record of the ancient Jewish historian Josephus, *The Jewish War*, which actually begins with the reign of Antiochus Ephiphanes. Several translations of this work are now available, including that in the Loeb Classical Library (10 vols. [Cambridge, Mass.: Harvard University Press, 1926-65]) and the more recent *Josephus: The*

164 How to Read the Gospels and Acts

Jewish War, ed. Gaalya Cornfeld et al. (Grand Rapids, Mich.: Zondervan, 1982).

[17]See the brief survey in my *How to Read Prophecy* (Downers Grove, Ill.: InterVarsity, 1984), pp. 61-65. For more technical introductions, see Stephen H. Travis, *Christian Hope and the Future* (Downers Grove, Ill.: InterVarsity, 1980), especially pp. 25-49; Paul D. Hanson, ed., *Visionaries and Their Apocalypses* (Philadelphia: Fortress, 1983).

[18]Paul D. Hanson, "Introduction," in *Visionaries and Their Apocalypses,* p. 3.

[19]In a groundbreaking essay, Ernst Käsemann wrote, "Apocalyptic was the mother of all Christian theology" ("The Beginnings of Christian Theology," in *New Testament Questions of Today* [Philadelphia: Fortress, 1969], p. 102). See now the studies by Travis (*Christian Hope,* pp. 41-49) and James D. G. Dunn (*Unity and Diversity in the New Testament* [Philadelphia: Fortress, 1977] pp. 316-40).

[20]See chapter eleven.

[21]See Joachim Jeremias, *Jerusalem in the Time of Jesus* (Philadelphia: Fortress, 1969); Schürer, *History;* Rowland, *Christian Origins,* pp. 65-75.

[22]That Jesus was able to do so, see Mt 22:23-33.

[23]See John Rogerson, "The World-View of the Old Testament," in *Beginning Old Testament Study,* ed. John Rogerson (Philadelphia: Westminster, 1982), pp. 55-73, especially pp. 56-58; Meyer, *Aims of Jesus,* pp. 159-60. For important analyses of this issue from the perspective of cultural anthropology, see especially Bruce J. Malina, *The New Testament World: Insights from Cultural Anthropology* (Atlanta: John Knox, 1981); *Christian Origins and Cultural Anthropology: Practical Models for Biblical Interpretation* (Atlanta: John Knox, 1986).

[24]Geoffrey Wainwright, *Eucharist and Eschatology* (London: Epworth, 1971), pp. 19-20.

[25]See also 1 Enoch 62:1-16; 2 Bar 29:5-8; 1 QSa 2:11-22; Wainwright, *Eucharist,* pp. 20-25.

[26]The problematic term ἐποιύσιν may be understood in this way—as acknowledged by the New English Bible and American Standard Version, to name two examples. For the debate, see Wainwright, *Eucharist,* pp. 30-34.

Chapter 4: The Gospels as Good News

[1]The generic question continues to be contested among scholars—see the recent survey in Robert Guelich, "The Gospel Genre," in *Das Evangelium und die Evangelien: Vorträge vom Tübinger Symposium 1982,* ed. Peter Stuhlmacher (Tübingen: J. C. B. Mohr [Paul Siebeck], 1983), pp. 183-219.

[2]See Gerhard Friedrich, "εὐαγγελίζομαι," in *Theological Dictionary of the New Testament,* 10 vols., eds. Gerhard Kittel and Gerhard Friedrich (Grand Rapids, Mich.: Eerdmans, 1964-76) 2:707-37; Carl R. Kazmierski, *Jesus, Son of God: A Study of the Markan Tradition and Its Redaction by the Evangelist* (Würzburg:

Echter, 1979), pp. 18-22.

[3]See Ernest Best, *Mark: The Gospel as Story* (Edinburgh: T. & T. Clark, 1983), p. 38.

[4]See Best, *Mark*, pp. 38-43. This idea was set forth by Willi Marxsen; see, for example, his *Introduction to the New Testament* (Philadelphia: Fortress, 1968), p. 138. With proper limits (see Best, *Mark*, pp. 39-41), this is a helpful descriptive term.

[5]Albert Schweitzer, *The Quest of the Historical Jesus: A Critical Study of Its Progress from Reimarus to Wrede*, 3d ed. (London: SCM, 1954).

[6]The identity of the third and fourth evangelists will be briefly discussed in chapter five. It should be noted that all four Gospels are anonymous.

[7]See the discussion in I. Howard Marshall, *The Gospel of Luke: A Commentary on the Greek Text* (Grand Rapids, Mich.: Eerdmans, 1978), pp. 99-104.

[8]From *Synopsis of the Four Gospels: Greek-English Edition of the Synopsis Quattuor Evangeliorum*, ed. Kurt Aland (United Bible Society, 1971), p. 344.

[9]See Edgar V. McKnight, *The Bible and the Reader: An Introduction to Literary Criticism* (Philadelphia: Fortress, 1985), p. xvii.

[10]For an evangelical assessment of these and other developments in exegetical method, see George Eldon Ladd, *The New Testament and Criticism* (Grand Rapids, Mich. Eerdmans, 1967); I. Howard Marshall, ed., *New Testament Interpretation. Essays on Principles and Methods* (Grand Rapids, Mich.: Eerdmans, 1977).

[11]Fred B. Craddock, *The Gospels* (Nashville: Abingdon, 1981), p. 26.

[12]For this emphasis in Luke, see Richard J. Cassidy, *Jesus, Politics, and Society: A Study of Luke's Gospel* (Maryknoll, N. Y.: Orbis, 1978), pp. 20-49; Robert F. O'Toole, *The Unity of Luke's Theology: An Analysis of Luke-Acts* (Wilmington, Del.: Michael Glazier, 1984), pp. 109-48.

[13]On this historical character of the Gospel of Luke, see chapter five.

[14]See Robert A. Guelich, "The Gospels: Portraits of Jesus and His Ministry," *Journal of the Evangelical Theological Society* 24 (1982): 117-25.

Chapter 5: The Gospels as History

[1]George Wesley Buchanan, *Jesus: The King and His Kingdom* (Macon, Ga.: Mercer University, 1984), p. 310: "When Jesus was captured, the apostles soon vanished. How, then, could later generations know how Jesus reacted to this time of suffering? What happened at the cross? How did Jesus respond, and what were his thoughts and feelings?" Buchanan answers that Matthew built up his passion story from Psalms 22 and 69. For a different treatment of the evidence, see my "The Death of Jesus."

[2]William Wrede, *The Messianic Secret* (London: James Clarke, 1971). For an introduction to the modern debate sparked by Wrede's treatment of the secrecy motif in Mark, see *The Messianic Secret*, ed. Christopher Tuckett (Philadelphia: Fortress, 1983).

[3]James Breech, *The Silence of Jesus: The Authentic Voice of the Historical Man* (Philadelphia: Fortress, 1983), p. 6.

[4]This need is well-emphasized by Paul J. Achtemeier, *The Inspiration of Scripture: Problems and Proposals* (Philadelphia: Westminster, 1980); and Marshall, *Biblical Inspiration.*

[5]Among the many monographs on the subject, see especially I. Howard Marshall, *I Believe in the Historical Jesus* (Grand Rapids, Mich.: Eerdmans, 1977).

[6]Many scholars hold that Matthew and Luke made use of a sayings-source designated as Q" (shorthand for the German word for "source," *Quelle?*). The theory regarding the existence of such documents has received support from the discovery of an example of this kind of document among the Nag Hammadi finds, *The Gospel of Thomas.* For a survey of the discussion, see Howard Biggs, "The Q Debate Since 1955," *Themelios* 6 (2, 1981):18-28.

[7]On what follows, see Heinz Schürmann, "Die vorösterlichen Anfänge der Logientradition: Versuch eines formgeschichtlichen Zugangs zum Leben Jesu," in *Traditionsgeschichtliche Untersuchungen zu den synoptischen Evangelien* (Düsseldorff: Patmos, 1968), pp. 39-65; Birger Gerhardsson, *The Origins of the Gospel Traditions* (Philadelphia: Fortress, 1977); Rainer Riesner, *Jesus als Lehrer: Eine Untersuchung zum Ursprung der Evangelien-Uberlieferung* (Tübingen: J. C. B. Mohr [Paul Siebeck], 1981).

[8]C. H. Dodd, *The Apostolic Preaching and Its Developments* (London: Hodder & Stoughton, 1936; reprint ed., Grand Rapids, Mich.: Baker, 1980).

[9]On the pre-Lukan character of this reference, see now Robert Guelich, "The Gospel Genre," pp. 209-11.

[10]For further evidence of this sort, see G. N. Stanton, *Jesus of Nazareth in New Testament Preaching* (Cambridge: Cambridge University, 1974).

[11]Stephen S. Smalley, *1, 2, 3 John* (Waco, Texas: Word, 1984), p. 15.

[12]Martin Hengel, "Literary, Theological and Historical Problems in the Gospel of Mark," in *Studies in the Gospel of Mark* (London: SCM, 1985), p. 41. See also Caird, *Language and Imagery,* p. 212; I. Howard Marshall, *Luke: Historian and Theologian* (Grand Rapids, Mich.: Zondervan, 1971), especially pp. 20-76.

[13]See chapters six and seven.

[14]In addition to the commentaries, see Robert L. Maddox, *The Purpose of Luke-Acts* (Edinburgh: T. & T. Clark, 1982), pp. 4-5; Marshall, *Luke: Historian and Theologian,* pp. 37-41; "Luke and His 'Gospel,' " in *Das Evangelium und die Evangelien,* pp. 295-96.

[15]See Maddox, *The Purpose of Luke-Acts,* pp. 3-6.

[16]See, for example, Thucydides *History of the Peloponnesian War* 1.22.2-3; Josephus *Against Apion* 55; Polybius *The Histories* 12.25e.

[17]For an extensive review of the evidence and a conclusion in favor of identifying the author of Luke-Acts with Luke, Paul's companion, see Joseph A.

Fitzmyer, *The Gospel according to Luke*, 2 vols. (Garden City, N.Y.: Doubleday, 1981-85) 1:35-53.

[18]See Marshall, *Historical Jesus*, p. 148; Maddox, *The Purpose of Luke-Acts*, p. 7.

[19]Marshall, *Gospel of Luke; The Acts of the Apostles: An Introduction and Commentary* (Grand Rapids, Mich.: Eerdmans, 1980); W. Ward Gasque, *A History of the Criticism of the Acts of the Apostles* (Tübingen: J. C. B. Mohr [Paul Siebeck], 1975).

[20]Thus, for example, Günther Bornkamm notes: "The Gospel according to John has so different a character in comparison with the other three, and is to such a degree the product of a developed theological reflection, that we can only treat it as a secondary source" *(Jesus of Nazareth* [London: Hodder and Stoughton, 1960], p. 14).

[21]C. H. Dodd, *Historical Tradition in the Fourth Gospel* (Cambridge: Cambridge University, 1963). See the even more hopeful view of D. A. Carson, "Historical Tradition in the Fourth Gospel: After Dodd, What?" in *Studies of History and Tradition in the Four Gospels,* Gospel Perspectives, vol. 2, ed. R. T. France and David Wenham (Sheffield: JSOT, 1981), pp. 83-145.

[22]E. Earle Ellis, *The World of St. John: The Gospel and the Epistles* (Nashville: Abingdon, 1965; reprint ed., Grand Rapids, Mich.: Eerdmans, 1984), p. 52. One of the more helpful studies for explaining the obvious differences in the way the sayings of Jesus appear in the Gospel of John is J. Ramsey Michaels, *Servant and Son: Jesus in Parable and Gospel* (Atlanta: John Knox, 1981). Michaels shows how many of the Christological images employed by the fourth evangelist may have originated in Synopticlike material.

Chapter 6: The Gospels as Theology

[1]Eduard Schweizer, *The Good News according to Mark* (Atlanta: John Knox, 1970), p. 340; Rudolf Pesch, *Das Markusevangelium*, vol. 2, 3d ed. (Freiburg: Herder, 1984), pp. 470-71.

[2]Philo *Flaccus* 6. 36-39.

[3]Plantagenet and Fiona Somerset Fry, *The History of Scotland* (London: Routledge & Kegan Paul, 1982), p. 182.

[4]See, above all, Stephen S. Smalley, *John: Evangelist and Interpreter* (Exeter: Paternoster, 1978). Also, Ellis, *The World of St. John.*

[5]The debate regarding the source of this declaration—namely, whether it first designated the conclusion of a "signs-source" (see Robert T. Fortna, *The Gospel of Signs* [Cambridge: Cambridge University, 1970])—need not detain us. Regardless of its derivation, the evangelist's use of it here must be taken seriously in this context.

[6]In fact, this is a text-critical problem, with many texts reading *you may believe,* while the better texts read *you may continue to believe.*

[7]Rudolf Schnackenburg, *The Gospel according to St. John,* vol. 3 (New York: Crossroad, 1982), pp. 338-39.

[8]See Marshall, *Luke: Historian and Theologian,* pp. 116-17.

[9]Smalley, *John: Evangelist and Interpreter,* p. 139.

[10]A helpful, if technical, resource for coming to terms with *The Interpretation of Matthew* has been edited by Graham Stanton (Philadelphia: Fortress, 1983). For commentary suggestions on the Gospels and Acts, see the Suggested Reading listed at the back of this book.

[11]Jack Dean Kingsbury, *Matthew: Structure, Christology, Kingdom* (Philadelphia: Fortress, 1975).

[12]These Old Testament citations sometimes cause problems for modern Christians who recognize the apparent freedom Matthew is taking with the Old Testament contexts of the passages he cites. On this see Green, *How to Read Prophecy,* chapter seven.

[13]Ralph P. Martin *(Mark: Evangelist and Theologian* [Grand Rapids, Mich.: Zondervan, 1972]) has provided a helpful introduction to the interpretation of the Second Gospel. More technical but quite useful are Howard C. Kee, *Community of the New Age: Studies in Mark's Gospel* (London: SCM, 1977); and William R. Telford, ed., *The Interpretation of Mark* (Philadelphia: Fortress, 1985).

[14]For a general discussion of Luke's purpose, see the introduction to Luke's purpose in Marshall, *Luke: Historian and Theologian.* More technical is Maddox, *The Purpose of Luke-Acts.* For discussion of Luke's social and political themes, see, for example, Cassidy, *Jesus, Politics, and Society;* Richard J. Cassidy and Philip J. Scharper, eds., *Political Issues in Luke-Acts* (Maryknoll, N.Y.: Orbis, 1983); J. Massyngbaerde Ford, *My Enemy Is My Guest: Jesus and Violence in Luke* (Maryknoll, N.Y.: Orbis, 1984). More balaced overall is O'Toole, *The Unity of Luke's Theology.*

Chapter 7: The Gospels as Story

[1]Peter E. Gillquist, *Let's Quit Fighting about the Holy Spirit* (Grand Rapids, Mich.: Zondervan, 1974), pp. 107-8.

[2]See James D. G. Dunn, *Baptism in the Holy Spirit: A Reexamination of the New Testament Teaching on the Gift of the Spirit in Relation to Pentecostalism Today* (Philadelphia: Westminster, 1970), pp. 38-54; *Jesus and the Spirit: A Study of the Religious and Charismatic Experience of Jesus and the First Christians as Reflected in the New Testament* (Philadelphia: Fortress, 1975), pp. 135-56; I. Howard Marshall, "The Significance of Pentecost," *Scottish Journal of Theology* 30 (1977): 347-69.

[3]Marshall, "Pentecost," p. 365.

[4]Dunn, *Jesus and the Spirit,* p. 153.

Chapter 8: Story-Telling in the Gospels

[1]In addition to the commentaries, see Marshall D. Johnson, *The Purpose of the Biblical Genealogies with Special Reference to the Setting of the Genealogies of*

Jesus (Cambridge: Cambridge University, 1969), especially pp. 139-228; Raymond E. Brown, *The Birth of the Messiah: A Commentary on the Infancy Narratives in Matthew and Luke* (Garden City, N.Y.: Doubleday, 1977), pp. 57-95. The theological import of Old Testament genealogies is briefly noted in John Barton, *Reading the Old Testament: Method in Biblical Study* (London: Darton, Longman and Todd, 1984), pp. 47-51.

[2]Brown, *Birth*, pp. 60-61.

[3]Robert H. Mounce, *Matthew* (San Francisco: Harper & Row, 1985), p. 2.

[4]The most convincing explanation for the significance of the number 14 still rests on the observation that the numerical value of the Hebrew letters in the name David (dwd) is 14 ($d = 4$, $w = 6$, $d = 4$). By this pattern, Jesus is revealed as the eschatological Son of David, the Messiah.

[5]A brief, if somewhat technical, introduction to apocalyptic literature is John J. Collins, *Daniel; with an Introduction to Apocalyptic Literature* (Grand Rapids, Mich.: Eerdmans, 1984), pp. 2-24.

[6]See Green, *How to Read Prophecy*, pp. 63-64.

[7]English translation from Bruce M. Metzger, "The Fourth Book of Ezra," in *The Old Testament Pseudepigrapha*, vol. 1: *Apocalyptic Literature and Testaments*, ed. James H. Charlesworth (Garden City, N.Y.: Doubleday, 1983), p. 535.

[8]See Norman Perrin, *The New Testament: An Introduction* (New York: Harcourt Brace Jovanovich, 1974), pp. 77-78.

[9]In fact, it seems highly probable for this reason that Mark 13 was composed from dominical material and received something of its present form in early Christian catechesis—see G. R. Beasley-Murray, "Second Thoughts on the Composition of Mark 13," *New Testament Studies* 29 (3, 1983):414-20.

[10]See Stephen H. Travis, *I Believe in the Second Coming of Jesus* (Grand Rapids, Mich.: Eerdmans, 1982), p. 79. Also, Green, *How to Read Prophecy*, chapter six.

[11]See Ethelbert Stauffer, *New Testament Theology* (London: SCM, 1955), pp. 344-47; James I. H. McDonald, *Kerygma and Didache: The Articulation of the Earliest Christian Message* (Cambridge: Cambridge University, 1980), pp. 73, 79, 86-87, 98-99.

[12]See the important study of *The Sermon on the Mount* by Robert A. Guelich (Waco, Texas: Word, 1982).

[13]Joachim Jeremias, *New Testament Theology*, vol. 1: *The Proclamation of Jesus* (New York: Charles Scribner's Sons, 1971), pp. 35-36.

[14]The use of *Abba* itself by Jesus has no precedent in the Jewish literature known to us, though there were other expressions used infrequently which denoted a high level of familiarity with God—see Dunn, *Jesus and the Spirit*, pp. 21-26.

[15]The literature associated with the Son of Man debate is enormous. Probably the most helpful introduction to the problems associated with this title is I. Howard Marshall, *The Origins of New Testament Christology* (Downers Grove,

Ill.: InterVarsity, 1976), chapter four.

[16]See Marshall, *Luke: Historian and Theologian*, pp. 72-73.

[17]See F. F. Bruce, "The Speeches in Acts—Thirty Years Later," in *Reconciliation and Hope: New Testament Essays on Atonement and Eschatology Presented to L. L. Morris on His 60th Birthday*, ed. Robert Banks (Grand Rapids, Mich.: Eerdmans, 1974), pp. 53-68; W. Ward Gasque, "The Speeches in Acts: Dibelius Reconsidered," in *New Dimensions in New Testament Study*, eds. Richard N. Longenecker and Merrill C. Tenney (Grand Rapids, Mich.: Zondervan, 1974), pp. 232-51.

[18]The importance of the Damascus-road experience for Paul has been underscored recently by Seyoon Kim, *The Origin of Paul's Gospel* (Grand Rapids, Mich.: Eerdmans, 1981).

Chapter 9: The Form of Jesus' Message

[1]Robert H. Stein, *The Method and Message of Jesus' Teaching* (Philadelphia: Westminster, 1978), pp. 7-33.

[2]Caird, *Language and Imagery*, p. 144.

[3]See Leonhard Goppelt, *Theology of the New Testament*, 2 vols. (Grand Rapids, Mich.: Eerdmans, 1981-82), 2:293-96.

[4]For more discussion on points of comparison, see Caird, *Language and Imagery*, pp. 145-49.

[5]Stein, *Method and Message*, p. 22.

[6]Norman Perrin, *The Kingdom of God in the Teaching of Jesus* (Philadelphia: Westminster, 1963); *Jesus and the Language of the Kingdom* (London: SCM, 1976); *Rediscovering the Teaching of Jesus* (New York: Harper & Row, 1967); Royce Gordon Gruenler, *New Approaches to Jesus and the Gospels: A Phenomenological and Exegetical Study of Synoptic Christology* (Grand Rapids, Mich.: Baker, 1982); Stein, *Method and Message*, see especially pp. 25-27.

[7]See Colin Brown, *Miracles and the Critical Mind* (Grand Rapids, Mich.: Eerdmans, 1984).

Chapter 10: Parables in Jesus' Teaching

[1]Sally Springer and Georg Deutsch *(Left Brain, Right Brain* [New York: W. H. Freeman, 1981], pp. 190-92) note the deficiency of our educational systems in fostering full development of the broad spectrum of human capabilities.

[2]The classification of parables is big business among New Testament scholars, and one need not read very far in the literature to discover the same parables being classified under different headings. In what follows, I have attempted to simplify the categorization of the parables for a less scholarly audience.

[3]Augustine *Quaestiones Evangeliorum* 2.19; cited in Michaels, *Servant and Son*, p. 94.

[4]New Testament scholars have suffered a backlash from attempts in the early

church to read the parables allegorically and have therefore largely denied the allegorical content of those stories. Caird (*Language and Imagery*, pp. 160-71) provides a helpful corrective. Happily, there is now a growing awareness that we cannot dismiss ipso facto any allegory from Jesus' parables.

[5]John Dominic Crossan, *The Dark Interval: Towards a Theology of Story* (Niles, Ill.: Argus, 1975), p. 56.

[6]Fee and Stuart, *How to Read the Bible for All Its Worth*, p. 123.

[7]Bailey, *Poet & Peasant*, p. 41.

[8]This is a point well made by Robert H. Stein, *An Introduction to the Parables of Jesus* (Philadelphia: Westminster, 1981), pp. 75-77.

[9]For an introductory overview of this approach, see Derek Tidball, *The Social Context of the New Testament: A Sociological Analysis* (Grand Rapids, Mich.: Zondervan, 1984). Gerd Theissen is a pioneer in this field; see, for example, his study of *The First Followers of Jesus: A Sociological Analysis of the Earliest Christianity* (London: SCM, 1978). Bailey (*Poet & Peasant*) has blazed the trail for understanding the parables in Luke's Gospel from the perspective of cultural analysis. Kee (*Community of the New Age*) uses an examination of cultural and social factors in his treatment of the Second Gospel.

[10]Michaels, *Servant and Son*, pp. 99-100.

Chapter 11: Jesus and the Kingdom of God

[1]See also 2 Timothy 4:8 and the textual variant in John 3:5.

[2]Jeremias, *New Testament Theology*, pp. 9-10, 97.

[3]G. R. Beasley-Murray, "Jesus and the Kingdom of God," *Catalyst* 12, no. 3, (1986): 1-2. Recent commentators are divided over whether this summary statement should be credited to Mark or to the tradition he made use of.

[4]Important developments and themes related to the rise of this anticipation are discussed in Green, *How to Read Prophecy*, chapters seven and nine.

[5]English translation in F. I. Andersen, "2 (Slavonic Apocalypse of) Enoch," in *The Old Testament Pseudepigrapha*, 1:192. This apocalypse probably dates from the late first century A.D., but with respect to this idea it is representative of similar, earlier literature—see Russell, *Method and Message*, chapter ten.

[6]Bruce Chilton has edited a collection of essays representing recent attempts to come to terms with Jesus' understanding of the kingdom—*The Kingdom of God in the Teaching of Jesus* (Philadelphia: Fortress, 1984). An insightful study has recently been made by I. Howard Marshall, "The Hope of the New Age: The Kingdom of God in the New Testament," *Themelios* 11, no. 1 (1985): 5-15. See also George Eldon Ladd, *The Presence of the Future: The Eschatology of Biblical Realism* (Grand Rapids, Mich.: Eerdmans, 1974); Hermann Ridderbos, *The Coming of the Kingdom* (Philadelphia: Presbyterian and Reformed, 1962); John Riches, *Jesus and the Transformation of Judaism* (New York: Seabury, 1980).

[7]Studies on how Jesus perceived the timetable of the kingdom are legion. For a brief history of the debate see Stein, *Method and Message*, pp. 65-68.

[8]Beasley-Murray, "Jesus and the Kingdom of God." He refers to the foundational exegetical work of A. M. Ambrozic, *The Hidden Kingdom* (Washington, D. C.: Catholic Biblical Association of America, 1972), pp. 3-45.

[9]Edward Schillebeeckx, *Jesus: An Experiment in Christology* (London: Collins, 1979), p. 189.

[10]For a more recent example of this identification, see Philip Edgcumbe Hughes, *Interpreting Prophecy* (Grand Rapids, Mich.: Eerdmans, 1976), p. 107.

[11]See, for example, Hans Küng, *The Church* (Garden City, N.Y.: Doubleday, 1976), pp. 124-35.

[12]Marshall, "Hope of a New Age," p. 12.

[13]See Marshall, *Origins of NT Christology*, chapter four.

[14]See the programmatic work of Seyoon Kim, *"The 'Son of Man ' as the Son of God* (Tübingen: J. C. B. Mohr [Paul Siebeck], 1983).

[15]See Beasley-Murray, "Jesus and the Kingdom of God."

Suggested Reading

More advanced and technical selections are given in the notes.

Gospel Synopses
Aland, Kurt, ed. *Synopsis of the Four Gospels.* United Bible Societies, 1971.
Throckmorton, Burton H., Jr. *Gospel Parallels: A Synopsis of the First Three Gospels.* New York: Thomas Nelson, 1967.

The World of Jesus
Bruce, F. F. *New Testament History.* Garden City, New York: Doubleday, 1969.
Jeremias, Joachim. *Jerusalem in the Time of Jesus.* Philadelphia: Fortress, 1969.
Lohse, Eduard. *The New Testament Environment.* Nashville: Abingdon, 1976.
Rowland, Christopher. *Christian Origins.* Minneapolis, Minnesota: Augsburg, 1985.

Jesus and the Gospels
Dunn, James D. G. *The Evidence for Jesus.* Philadelphia: Westminster, 1985.
Marshall, I. Howard. *I Believe in the Historical Jesus.* Grand Rapids, Michigan: Eerdmans, 1977.

The Teaching of Jesus
Bailey, Kenneth E. *Poet and Peasant* and *Through Peasant Eyes.* Combined Edition. Grand Rapids, Michigan: Eerdmans, 1983.
Michaels, J. Ramsey. *Servant and Son: Jesus in Parable and Gospel.* Atlanta: John Knox, 1981.

174

Stein, Robert H. *The Method and Message of Jesus' Teaching.* Philadelphia: Westminster, 1978.

Stein, Robert H. *An Introduction to the Parables of Jesus.* Philadelphia: Westminster, 1981.

Commentaries and Special Studies
The Gospel of Matthew

Guelich, Robert A. *The Sermon on the Mount: A Foundation for Understanding.* Waco, Texas: Word, 1982.

Hill, David. *The Gospel of Matthew.* Grand Rapids, Michigan: Eerdmans, 1972.

Mounce, Robert H. *Matthew: A Good News Commentary.* San Francisco: Harper & Row, 1985.

The Gospel of Mark

Best, Ernest. *Mark: The Gospel as Story.* Edinburgh: T. & T. Clark, 1983.

Hurtado, Larry W. *Mark: A Good News Commentary.* San Francisco: Harper & Row, 1983.

Lane, William L. *The Gospel according to Mark.* Grand Rapids, Michigan: Eerdmans, 1974.

Martin, Ralph. *Mark: Evangelist and Theologian.* Grand Rapids, Michigan: Zondervan, 1972.

Pallares, José Cárdenas. *A Poor Man Called Jesus: Reflections on the Gospel of Mark.* Maryknoll, New York: Orbis, 1986.

The Gospel of Luke

Ellis, E. Earle. *The Gospel of Luke.* Rev. ed. Grand Rapids, Michigan: Eerdmans, 1974.

Cassidy, Richard J. *Jesus, Politics, and Society: A Study of Luke's Gospel.* Maryknoll, New York: Orbis, 1978.

Fitzmyer, Joseph A. *The Gospel according to Luke.* 2 vols. Garden City, New York: Doubleday, 1981/85.

Marshall, I. Howard. *Luke: Historian and Theologian.* Grand Rapids, Michigan: Zondervan, 1971.

The Gospel of John

Brown, Raymond E. *The Gospel according to John.* 2 vols. Garden City, New York: Doubleday, 1966.

Bruce, F. F. *The Gospel of John.* Grand Rapids, Michigan: Eerdmans, 1983.

Ellis, E. Earle. *The World of St. John: The Gospel and the Epistles.* Grand Rapids, Michigan: Eerdmans, 1984.

Lindars, Barnabas. *The Gospel of John.* Grand Rapids, Michigan: Eerdmans, 1972.

Smalley, Stephen S. *John: Evangelist and Interpreter.* Exeter: Paternoster, 1978.

The Acts of the Apostles

Bruce, F. F. *Commentary on the Book of the Acts.* Grand Rapids, Michigan: Eerd-mans, 1954.

Marshall, I. Howard. *The Acts of the Apostles.* Grand Rapids, Michigan: Eerd-mans, 1980.

Scripture Index